MW01152695

Whh Rose

WEAVER ROSE
(W. H. H. ROSE)

THE
WEAVING
ROSES

OF RHODE ISLAND

ISADORA M. SAFNER

INTERWEAVE PRESS

ABOUT THE AUTHOR: Isadora Safner lives on Cape Cod Bay with her husband, sons and bullmastiff, Samson. She has studied at Barnard College, Columbia University and Rhode Island School of Design. She is a pattern weaver by nature, and finds researching well-known weavers fascinating. She combines her varied interests by operating a weaving business and republishing books on well-known weavers.

ISBN 0-934026-19-X
Library of Congress card catalog number 85-82321.
Published by Interweave Press, Inc., 306 North Washington Avenue, Loveland, Colorado 80537.   5000:JLP, 12-85.

·CONTENTS·

"We have a tradition which is carried on by thoughts and words: has it been remarked that tradition is also carried on by things? Wheat itself is tradition, and good bread is tradition; not without reason have the great religions honored the breaking of bread together. Perhaps it would be well for us to recognize this body of tradition which lies in things and be more aware of it. We have grown blind to it and forget that apart from words it binds human being to human being, and that a way of life must seek to preserve the strengths whose roots go deep."

Henry Beston

Reprinted by permission of the Stephen Greene Press from *Especially Maine* by Henry Beston. Copyright 1970 by Elizabeth Coatsworth Beston.

·INTRODUCTION·

Dr. Donnell Brooks Young presented me with a manila envelope in 1983, with this admonition: ". . . do something with it." In it was a collection of hand-copied drafts entitled *Weaver Rose Patterns.* It was the collected drafts of Weaver Rose, William Henry Harrison Rose, the most well known of New England weavers. To me, this was an astounding surprise. Here was a treasury of early American weaving patterns. Also in the envelope was the correspondence of both Weaver Rose and his sister, Elsie Maria Babcock Rose, with Laura Allen of Rochester, New York. Their letters were not only about weaving, but were also a chronicle of their lives and the times in which they lived. They depicted a way of life long gone, one well worth retelling.

William Henry Harrison Rose was born well into the machine age of 1839. He and Elsie chose not to be a part of that era of industrialization, and for that all handweavers must be grateful. In the late nineteenth century, Weaver Rose began collecting weaving drafts, some of which date back to the 1700s. The establishment of a correspondence between him and Laura Allen about 1910 assured that the drafts would be preserved.

Laura Allen was an instructor in basketry and weaving at the Mechanics Institute in Rochester, New York, now the Rochester Institute of Technology-School for American Craftsmen. She taught there from 1911 through 1918. She was an excellent weaver, and a collector of textiles, three hundred pieces of which can now be found in the Smithsonian Institution. Mrs. Allen was one of the first collectors and collators of American weaving drafts. Her correspondence covered the country. One weaver would put her in contact with another, and from these multiple exchanges, she built her scrapbooks of drafts. She paid for some of these, including the Rose drafts, and she promised a royalty payment from a projected draft book to other weavers. She was the inspiration and fountainhead for work done by Mary Meigs Atwater and Marguerite Davison. The pattern book which she planned was never published.

After Mrs. Allen's death, Mrs. Davison acquired her papers and scrapbooks, and subsequently published *A Handweaver's Pattern Book* and *A*

Handweaver's Source Book. In these efforts she was aided by Helen Daniels Young (Mrs. Donnell Brooks Young). At Mrs. Davison's sudden death in 1953, the Allen collection was purchased from her estate by Dr. George Pariseau, who passed it on to Dr. and Mrs. Donnell Young. Thus this small group of very active, devoted weavers preserved the Allen collection, and made this book possible.

Weaver Rose's drafts were also collected by Mrs. Emily Beals of Abington, Pennsylvania. She found some of his originals at the home of Mrs. Grant LaFarge of Saunderstown, Rhode Island. They had come into Mrs. LaFarge's keeping after Elsie Rose's death. Mrs. Beals and Kate Van Cleve of Boston, a well known weaver and weaving teacher, had actively contemplated a book about WHHR in 1937. Some of the original drafts are now in the possession of Norma Smayda of Saunderstown, Rhode Island.

The drafts are well worth modern interpretation and use, for some are truly beautiful. In the context of their times and the lives of the Roses, they command a deep appreciation of our weaving heritage.

I.S.
Cape Cod, 1985

·HISTORY·

William Henry Harrison Rose was born on June 18, 1839, and died November 9, 1913. Few knew his whole name; most knew him as Weaver Rose or Quaker Billy Rose. Weaver Rose must be understood more as a product of his past than of the century in which he lived. The tales of his ancestors are those of the very founding of this Republic. His pride in their feats and his own way of life made him much more a man of the early nineteenth century than of the twentieth, when his country emerged as the leader of the industrial world. He was an anachronism: a living link between the rural Colonial-Revolutionary past, and the urban, industrialized present.

It is an irony of history that the Puritans, who had fled English persecution, in turn would neither tolerate any other church in their midst, nor dissent within their own church. This intolerance was responsible for the settlement of Rhode Island. Roger Williams, a former minister of a Puritan church in Salem, Massachusetts, rebelled against the church leaders who were also leaders of the colony. There were two points of contention between them: only church members could vote, and yet everyone in the community, member or no, had to pay Church taxes and attend services. Since the Puritans had no claim to the land which now makes up Rhode Island (it was regarded as belonging to the Indians), it became a refuge for all seeking to worship freely. Thus in 1636, Roger Williams and five followers were welcomed to that area by the Narragansett sachem (chief) Canonicus, and given land for a settlement. Likewise the Quakers, who were not welcome in Boston in 1656, came there. By the end of the seventeenth century, Rhode Island was populated largely with Baptists and Quakers.

Weaver Rose was a member of the fifth generation of his family in this country. Because the history of the counry is so intimately intertwined with those generations, some general history and background on Colonial-Indian relationships is pertinent. In 1636 the land of southern New England belonged to the Algonquian language-speaking peoples. Their individual groups were designated by the dialects each spoke: Wampanoag, Natick, Nauset, Nipmuch, Pennacook, Mohegan, Pocumtuck, and others. Out of a total New England population of 27,450 in 1600, the Narragansett Indians of Rhode Island were the largest single entity, consisting of 4000 men, women and children.[1] They were generally on cordial terms with the English Governor at Boston, and the Roger Williams group in Rhode Island. They deeded lands to the colonists on many occasions, but there was a basic difference in the Indian and English-Colonial perception of the "deed". To the Indian, a deed meant the right to use the land jointly; under English law, though, a deed meant sole ownership, and "by deed" meant not as a gift and/or King's commission, or by war. Thus, starting in 1657 and again in 1660 and 1661, and each time extended, the Petaquamscut Land Purchases by deed were made by Messrs. Wilbur, Hull, Potter, Mumford, and Wilson.[2]

Petaquamscut, or Pesquamscot, is an Indian place name in the Narragansett dialect for a river and pond in Washington County, the 'South County' of the Narragansett Bay region of Rhode Island. The word itself means, in suggested translation, "at the cleft rock" or "split boulder place".[3] The Petaquamscut Land Purchase is an important part of the Weaver Rose story, for it was on land acquired in this purchase that the Rose farm was located, and where also a great tragedy in American history occurred. This was the Great Swamp Fight between the United Colonies of New England vs. the Narragansett Indians.

As earlier indicated, the Narragansetts enjoyed friendly relationships with the colonists. This was not true of other Indian groups, particularly the Wampanoags. The Narragansetts had been asked by the Wampanoags to take in and shelter some of their women, children and wounded men. The Narragansetts had done this, and therefore angered the English who were smarting from a defeat by the Wampanoags at Hadley, Massachusetts. Thus, on November 2, 1675, for "relieving and succouring Wampanoag women, children, and wounded men" and not delivering them up to the English, and also because they "did in a very reproachful and blasphemous manner, triumph and rejoice" over the English defeat at Hadley[4], one thousand soldiers were sent to enter Narragansett country unless the Narragansett sachem gave up the Wampanoag fugitives. The Narragansett sachem, Cononchet, refused, and with all other Narragansett sachems except Ninigret, retired to a fortified island located in the middle of the Great Swamp in South Kingstown. There were

---

[1]J.C. Huden, *Indian Place Names of New England*, New York: Museum of the American Indian, Heye Foundation, 1962.
[2]S.S. Rider, *The Lands of Rhode Island as They Were Known to Caunounicus and Miantunnomu When Roger Williams Came in 1636*. Providence, R.I.: published by the author.
[3]Huden.
[4]H.M. Chapin, *Sachems of the Narragansetts*, Rhode Island: R.I. Historical Society, 1931.

only two means of closely guarded access. The battle was set, and on Saturday, November 18, 1675, two English contingents joined forces at Petaquamscut. Overnight the pond froze, allowing the English easy approach to the island, and the battle, "amidst ice, snow, underbrush, and fallen trees," began.[5] By noon, the English reached the fort where they set fire to six hundred wigwams housing women, children, wounded warriors, and old men. The Indians retreated. The English sustained losses of five captains, twenty men, and one hundred-fifty wounded. On the return march they lost thirty or forty more men. The Indian losses were forty fighting men, one sachem, and three hundred old men, women, and children burned alive in wigwams.[6] This was the Great Swamp Fight. Weaver Rose's great, great grandfather Eldred is though to have killed the Indian warrior Hunewell after the Swamp Fight at Silver Spring, about two miles from the Rose home. In that encounter, Eldred escaped from another warrior, but never forgot his face. Some years later, recognizing him in Newport, as Weaver Rose told it, "Grandfather got an awl and settled it in his forehead and finished him."[7]

Records show that other Rose ancestors were members of the provincial assemblies. Great grandfather Robert Northrup was commissioned a captain of the Second Company of North Kingstown in King's County of May 12, 1747, and died in 1783. The commission was made under King George III and came into the possession of Weaver Rose. Four great uncles were involved in the Revolution; two were taken on board ship by a Yankee privateer and brought to Dartmoor Prison in England, where their story ends. The third great uncle died of starvation aboard the prison ship Jersey. The fourth perished while imprisoned by the British in Newport, Rhode Island. The son of one of the great uncles to be imprisoned in Dartmoor in the Revolution was captured in the War of 1812 and spent eight years in Dartmoor. He then returned to Wickford, Rhode Island, and assumed an administrative office in that town for the remainder of his life. Rowland Robinson Rose, Weaver Rose's father, also fought in the War of 1812.[8] On the Rose side of the family, one ancestor is thought to have come from France and to have been known as the Duke of the Golden Rose. His coat of arms was reported to have borne a yellow rose.[9]

---

[5]Chapin, p. 80.
[6]Chapin, p. 81.
[7]A.M. Earle, *In Old Narragansett*. New York: Charles Scribner's Sons, 1898. p. 40.
[8]Earle, p. 39.
[9]Weaver Rose was alleged also to be a relative of President William McKinley and the wife of Theodore Roosevelt. She visited him and bought some rugs and a coverlet in the "World Wonder" pattern. An autographed photo of President Roosevelt in his Rough Rider uniform was accorded a prominent place on the Rose's parlor mantlepiece.

Weaver Rose's farming skills and fierce patriotism came from the Rose and Northrup men, and his weaving inheritance came directly from the Northrups and Austins on the maternal side of the family tree. His maternal great grandparents were in the weaving business. Great grandfather Austin was a wool sorter, and Great grandmother Austin a weaver. Their daughter Mary, a weaver and weaving teacher of some note, married Robert Northrup, also a weaver. Their daughter, Anstis, was the mother of Weaver Rose. It was the Austins who were Quakers. Great grandmother Austin was one of sixteen children: Parvis, Picus, Piersus, Prisemus, Polybius, Lois, Lettice, Avis, Anstice, Eunice, Mary, John, Elizabeth, Ruth, and Freelove. All lived to be seventy, and one to be a hundred and two years old.[10] At this point, it is important to sketch out this weaving heritage for its broad historical interest, as well as for how it pertains to Weaver Rose and Elsie.

In the late eighteenth century in the Narragansett region of Rhode Island, there were many handweavers: judges, minister's sons, and Martin Read, the "Prince of Narragansett weavers".[11] He was an orphan, apprenticed to a diaper-weaver at the age of seven. He served his weaver's training until he came of age, with only one term of schooling. In 1761 he was baptized in St. Paul's Church as "Martin Read, an adult, the Parrish Clerk", and served the Church for many years. During the Revolutionary War he read the morning prayers and the funeral service for the dead. He married the daughter of an Irish weaver. As a weaver, he took on apprentices and journeymen, one of whom was Robert Northrup, the maternal grandfather of Weaver Rose. The Read weaving establishment produced coverlets, blankets, broadcloch, flannel, worsted, linen, and calamanco, a twilled worsted fabric used for clothing by the more affluent citizens of the day. Also produced was crocus, a coarse towcloth for clothing which servants might wear. Martin Read died in 1822.

Robert Northrup and his wife, Mary, were described to Mrs. Earle in a letter from Weaver Rose written, at the latest, in 1898:

> My grandfather and grandmother Robert and Mary Northrup lived at what is now called Stuart Vale but then known as the Fish Pond, in a little hamlet of four houses, only one of which my grandfathers, is now standing. He owned a shore and fished in the spring and wove some at home and went out amongst the larger farmers working at his trade of weaving, whilst his wife carried on

---

[10]Earle, p. 40.
[11]Earle, p. 29.

the weaving at home and had a number of apprentices. He learned his trade of weaving of Martin Read, the deacon of St. Paul's church, who lived a few rods from the church. He died in 1822; his wife lived till 1848. The spool I gave you was made by Landworthy Pierce, a veteran of the Revolution. It has the initials of his name. I send you now one of his shuttles used for weaving broadcloth, and a square of linen I have woven for you of a pattern of five harnesses called Browbey. The looms here in Narragansett were all made by local carpenters. Stephen Northrup made looms, and Freeborn Church made looms and spinning wheels. I have 2 of his make. Friend Earle! more money can be made by weaving than farming. I have wove 30 yards of rag carpet in one day at 10 cents a yard; or 23 cents per yard when I found the warp. There was a man here by the name of Eber Sherman, he called himself Slippery Eber. He died in the War of 1812; his widow worked at spinning for 25 cents per day and supported herself and one son well on that wage. One dollar and a half per week was regular wage for a woman's work. It took a woman one week to weave a coverlet of 3 yards long and 2½ yards. Mahala Douglas went out to work at one dollar and a half per week making butter and cheese, milking seven cows every week day and nine on Sunday. She died leaving a large Estate, several thousand dollars, which her Legatees had no trouble in spending in six weeks. My grandfather was one of eight children. One brother was Rev. William Northrup; Thurston Northrup, another brother, was a school-teacher and a weaver of coverlets and cloth. John Northrup was called Weaver John. He was a coverlet weaver. John Congdon was a maker of Weavers' reeds or slays. I have 70 or 80 of his make in my house. I have a reed that my grandfather Northrup had made when he went to the Island of Rhode Island and weaving Broadcloth. He received 50 centers per day pay. Good Cream Cheese was 3 cents a pound at the same time of the Embargo in the war of 1812. I have an Eight and Twenty slay with 29 Beer that cost one dollar, made by John Congdon 70 years ago, as good as when made. He lived in North Kingston.[12]

---

[12]Reprinted by permission of Charles Scribner's Sons from *In Old Narragansett* by Alice Morse Earle, 1898. Pp. 36-37.

William Henry Harrison Rose and Elsie Maria Babcock Rose were the only two of the six Rose children, four girls and two boys, who took to the family trade of weaving. Weaver Rose's lifestyle, which he uncompromisingly pursued, was that of a professional weaver who lived his entire life in the family home, his birthplace, and who sustained himself and his sister from the land on which they lived. Described by Mrs. Earle in 1898, Weaver Rose was of "pale skin, hair and beard previously light brown, long and white." It flowed in waves over his shoulders and chest. His eyes were bright blue, and, from a sketch made in 1905, it is known that he wore glasses. He was slight of build and wore a collarless, short sleeved natural-colored wool shirt and overalls. He always walked with a long stick. A trip to town was described retrospectively in 1939 as follows:

> Once a week or 10 days he would pick up his long stick and with a quick, short step, start out, barefoot if the ground was not frozen for a basketful of supplies and snuff. Snuff was one of his most frequently used and necessary articles of equipment. Every story had to begin with the taking of an elaborate pinch of snuff. Thin and alert, with a long flowing white beard and snow-white hair showing beneath a wide-brimmed straw hat, 'Quaker Billy' was one of the few remaining types of a generation long past.[13]

When once asked if he was a religious person, Weaver Rose answered, "As religious as a Quaker can be."† A Kingston man, a contemporary of Weaver Rose's, said in an interview,

> The weaver is an interesting character. He's got ideas on health, takes a cold water bath every morning the year round and wears shoes only in the winter. When he meets you he offers you snuff — he's always taking snuff as another man would offer you a cigarette."[14]

The Rose homestead was build in 1816 on land dating back to the Petaquamscut land purchase. Located in the South County, Narragansett Bay region of Rhode Island, it was situated halfway between Slocum and Kingston, near a crossroads where the three towns of North Kingstown, South Kingstown, and Exeter meet.

---

[13]"R.I. State Girls Use Oaken Loom of Weaver Rose", *The Providence Evening Bulletin*, February 17, 1939.
[14]*The Providence Journal*, October 8, 1905, p. 24.
†As quoted in *Shuttle, Spindle & Dyepot* (see bibliography).

"Quaker Billy" Rose, about 1910. Courtesy of the Little Rest Archives, Kingston Free Library.

The house itself was in Exeter. It is interesting to note that at this crossroads a quaint custom was performed for the last time: a shift marriage. In a shift marriage, a widow clad only in her shift (slip), no matter what the season, would cross the King's highway three times and then be remarried on the spot. In so doing, she discharged herself of any debts that a previous husband had incurred. This custom was also known in New York and Pennsylvania.

The foundation of the Rose house was built by John R. Sherman, and the superstructure by Rowland Robinson Rose, Weaver Rose's father. The architecture was that of a 'full Cape'. The full Cape is often referred to as a "double house", with a door in the center and two windows on either side. In an

The Rose home. Courtesy of the Little Rest Archives, Kingston Free Library.

antique Cape house, there was on either side of the front door a room: to the right, the parlor, to the left, a bedroom. An open kitchen-dining room and possibly a borning room ran across the rear of the house. A central chimney provided each room with a fireplace. The hearth in the kitchen would have been quite large to accommodate cooking vessels, and would also have had some sort of oven, possibly a beehive type, built into the brickwork.

The Rose home grew to have a two story ell added onto the rear of the house. The first floor of the ell connected the house and barn, and the second floor housed the weaving loft. A narrow flight of stairs, opposite the front door, led to the second floor. In Weaver Rose's lifetime, the upper floor of the house contained his bedroom, with the remainder of the floor devoted to the weaving profession.

This weaving loft held three looms, one to each room. One loom was built by Weaver Rose from native cherry and sassafras wood. One, a hundred years old in 1905, was built by John Clarke of South Kingstown, and was given to Weaver Rose in 1880. On this one he wove mostly rugs, especially in the spring. The third loom was the one on which he wove the most; it was not very old, possibly thirty or forty years old in 1905. All three were of mid-eighteenth century design, huge, with an overhead beater. One had a loom seat on the frame, one a pulpit bench.

A large spinning wheel built by Freeborn Church, possibly a walking wheel, was used by the Rose family. A quill wheel used daily to wind quills was built in 1815. Weaver Rose had the shuttle described in the first patent ever taken out on a hand loom, a loom which made it possible to weave twenty yards of cotton in one day. His Aunt Hannah Northrup had the patented loom, possibly a flying shuttle loom. She lived in Stuartsville: "Lived right where Gilbert Stuart was born, and never heard of him," according to Weaver Rose.

In addition to the weaving tools used routinely by Weaver Rose, the weaving loft contained a collection of weaving paraphernalia dating through several generations. Under the rafters were several other spinning wheels, including one flax wheel used by his aunt Eunice for sixty-two years. There were shuttles, locally made and initialed by the carver, niddy-noddies, temples, Grandfather Northrup's heddle frames, swifts, harnesses, and carders. The following is an eyewitness description of the weaving loft.

Heaps of gay woollon yarns lay under the eaves, and a roll or two of rag-carpeting and strips of worn-out bed-coverlets of various patterns were hung on the beams or piled in heaps. There were vast boxes of cotton twine; and many yarn-beams ready wound, and swifts and quilling-wheels and "scarnes", many in number, thrust under the garret eaves. Among the discarded wool-wheels and flax wheels heaped high in the corner — obsolete before their fellow, the hand-loom . . . and the weaver, pale and silent, laboriously weaving his slow-growing web with a patience of past ages of workers, a patience so foreign to our present . . . that he seemed a century old, the very spirit of colonial . . . days.[15] [16]

---

[15]Earle, p. 31.

[16]In February of 1931, wind-fanned sparks from a train engine ignited a fire which spread rapidly. Its victim was the Rose house, deserted since Elsie's death. Burnt in its entirety, only the chimney remained. A curious piece from the *Narragansett Times* of February 13, 1931, concludes:

"Perhaps it was in keeping that the old house, so many years his refuge and home should be reduced to ashes as he had desired for his own earthly tenement."

At the time of Weaver Rose's death on November 9, 1913, only two siblings remained: Mrs. Hannah Sweet Sherman, age 91, and Elsie. Elsie was the last to survive and died on May 14, 1926, at 88 years of age. The way of life that Weaver Rose and Elsie chose necessitated a certain reclusiveness. Weaving and farming both take a great amount of time and hard labor. This is not to say that brother and sister were not fully cognizant of the changes taking place in the world around them. From time to time there were visitors, especially in the summer, and journeys were undertaken from the farm to the surrounding countryside and up to Providence.

The industrial age of weaving made its debut in New England in 1813 with the advent of the "first factory in America (if not the world), where a power loom was used and spinning and weaving were carried on under the same roof."[17] By the time Weaver Rose was at the height of his career, the growth in manufactured yarns and fabrics was well underway. He found it necessary to adapt his business to be competitive, since mill goods were less costly, and therefore the market available to the handweaver was greatly diminished. He accomplished this in several ways. His weaving was done to order, custom weaving. He used coarser yarns both for the cotton warp and tabby, and for the wool pattern weft. These coarse yarns cut down on the time necessary to dress the loom and weave the goods. He ordered the yarns either at the Kingston general store, or from the mill directly. He advertised in a monthly newspaper, *The Weaver's Herald*, Lyons, Kansas, 1899, volume viii, numbers 1 & 2:

The use of the word 'hap-harlot' is especially interesting, as it was certainly not in common parlance, and according to Alice Morse Earle, had not been seen in weaving literature since Holinshed's 1570 *Chronicles of*

---

[17]At Waltham, Massachusetts, by Messrs. Lowell, Jackson, and Moody. A. Barlow, *The History and Principles of Weaving*. London: Sampson, Low, Searle, and Rivington, 1879. p. 45.

Elsie Rose with her horse, Pinky. Courtesy of the Little Rest Archives, Kingston Free Library.

England. She writes, though, that in 1898 in Narragansett, weavers used the 300 year old term.[18] It is certainly one that would catch the imagination in an advertisement, or on the business card which Weaver Rose also had printed. All the advertised products, hap-harlot or coarse coverlets, portieres or door covers, bathroom rugs, rag rugs, pillow tops, and couch covers, were done from patterns nearly a hundred years old in 1898.

Over a period of many years, it was the fashion for wealthy summer residents of the Narragansett Bay region, Wickford, Narragansett Pier, and Saunderstown, to take a trip to the charming Rose homestead to meet 'Quaker Billy' and Elsie. If he happened to be hoeing in a field, Elsie would pick up a conch shell and blow into it. He would come on the run. Weaver Rose was not unaware of the charm of the rose-surrounded house and all the curiosities it contained. He would take the time to explain the relics in the weaver's loft. Owen Wister, the author, was a frequent guest, and bought hundreds of dollars worth of weaving. Then there was a Boston gentleman for whom

---

[18]Earle, p. 34.

Weaver Rose wove material for two waistcoats: one, a blue and green all-over design, and a second in scarlet wool and cotton, in the "Flowers of Canaan" pattern. One wealthy Narragansett Pier lady left him a piece of ribbon from her garter as a color guide for her couch cover. That was strong stuff in 1905! Our Weaver Rose was quite a salesman! Payment was required at the placement of an order, or the goods were sent C.O.D.

Weaver Rose was also an erstwhile poet with an eye to his profession. He wrote the following, in which the use of capitals and spelling run true to his form.

> come ye Patrones Proud and Lowley
> Rich and Raged, Every Man
> Come and Fork over what you owe
> The poor old weaver Man.
> We are rite Anxious to Receive it
> Oh, we Sadley Nead the Chink,
> Every Dollar Bright Believe It
> To Pay for Weaving Warp and Wullen.
> Pray Dont hesitate ye byers
> Of the Weavers Pittance Think
> Send o Send the Silver Shiners
> Quickly Cash us or We Sink.[19]

What is it that distinguishes Weaver Rose from any other well known American weaver? What is his legacy to contemporary weavers? The Roses lived a life that some would call "simple". Their neighbors thought them eccentric. He plied his trade as a lone craftsman, took orders from samples, ordered the yarns, and wove the finished products. Brother and sister tended their farm, fields and animals, and grew the crops which sustained them year round. However, Weaver Rose was far from a simple man. He *chose* to pursue and preserve a former way of life, a life fast disappearing from the American scene. He personified the tradition of the solitary American weaver, but beyond this, he looked to the future. He honored and used that which had gone before: the

---

[19] *The Providence Journal*, October 8, 1905. p. 24.

vocabulary, the tools, and especially the drafts. The drafts were not only those of his grandparents, but all of those which he could collect from weavers throughout the country. He offered to pay for those he collected and was recompensed for his own. He shared his knowledge and collection willingly.

Perhaps the greatest gift from this shy, retiring man to all weavers was his attempt to form an organization of American weavers. He was ill—the "sick spells" mentioned later in the Allen correspondence from 1910-1913—but he was determined not to let his life's work pass with him. He issued invitations to a small group of handweavers to meet at his home on September 2, 1912. Of the seven guests present, at least six can be identified: William and Elsie Rose, Laura Allen, Mr. E.D. Chapman, Mrs. Arnold Talbot, and Mrs. Wallace.[20] They did, indeed, form an organization called "The Colonial Weavers Association"; and elected Weaver Rose as their first and, as it turned out, only president, over his objections.

The stated objective of the Association was to encourage handweaving as an art as well as a handicraft. The afternoon was spent discussing different patterns, and subjects of interest to weavers. Though a national organization of weavers did not develop until much later, this was Weaver Rose's attempt to insure the future of American handweaving, by solidifying communication between the practitioners of the art and craft which consumed his entire life.

---

[20]From Weaver Rose's correspondence with Laura Allen, November 21, 1912, and Elsie's correspondence, January 25, 1914. See pages 20 and 24.

Kingston R I 8th mo 1911

I received yours Containing
the Names of the patterns
I do Not want them For Nothing
But will make recompence
you can Send those
Without Name Si 2 or 3
you think the handest
I will weave a Square
And Send you take your
time For the others
  W h h Rose
  Kingston R I

Facsimile of a letter written by Weaver Rose to Laura Allen in August, 1911.

·CORRESPONDENCE·

Weaver Rose corresponded with Laura Allen from May 10, 1910, to August 21, 1913 three months before his death. The letters are written in pencil and pen on lined paper, folded to a size of five inches wide and six inches tall. He used no punctuation, and an arbitrary use of capitals is very evident. When using pencil, he indeed seems to accent the capitals or numbers to emphasize a point. Some of the letters are written on every other line.

The occasional use of editorial brackets is to indicate a missing letter, as is the use of dots to indicate an undecipherable word or deletion in the letter. No salutation is used in any of Weaver Rose's correspondence. The dating differs from Elsie's: WHHR, "Kingston RI 10th mo 5th 1910", and EMBR, "Kingston RI Sept 13 1912".

These letters are reproduced as written, the number of words to the line exact, spelling and punctuation also exact. The original writing is longhand.

Kingston RI 10th mo 5th 1910
I received yours will Try To
how to begin to draw
draw one thred on the First
Shaft[1] then one on the
Second Shaft that makes 2
then one of the First Shaft
makes 3 one on the Second that is 4
I rote you all I Know
About Abreham Mellors
Book[2] he Published and
Charged $100 But could
Not Sell at that Price
he advertised I[n] the wevers
herald Published In
Lyons Kansas
I have been Very Sick

Since I rote you or I
Should made you Some
Pillow tops
If there is aney thing
I can Show you about
Weaving I am willing
to I have Figgerd your
Drafts and put them in
My Shape there is a mis
In the one Called Rose Leaf
Bud
If there is aney patern
I have you want I will
Send What is the price of
The Book published in 1817
I wood Like to get one
        W h h Rose

---

[1]It is of interest that WHHR uses the term 'shaft' here rather than 'harness'. The use of the former is usually British and the latter American. The Bronsons used the term 'harness' in their book, which was probably the one referred to in this letter as "The book published in 1817." Its complete title is *The Domestic Manufacturer's Assistant, and Family Directory In The Arts of Weaving and Dyeing.*

[2]The Abreham Mellors book was most likely offered for sale at $1.00, not the figure of $100 that the unpunctuated letter seems to suggest. From Mrs. Allen's draft collection, the correct spelling is Abraham Mellor. The draft is dated 1892, which may have been the date of the book. A single postcard bears the message, written by another hand, "Book received alright." It is signed in WHHR's hand, "W h h Roose". Postmarked Dec 21 with no year, it could have referred to the Mellor book discussed in this October 5 letter.

Kingston R I 8th mo 1911

I received yours Containing
the Names of the paterns
I do Not want them For Nothing
But will make recompense
you can Send those
Without Name Sen 2 or 3
you think the handest
I will weave a Square
And Send you take your
time For the others
    W h h Rose
    Kingston R I
    Box 63

[List of drafts on inside of letter][3]

Crossewise

Isaac Favorite
The Parsons Beauty
Square & Diamonds
Alabama Beauty
Rose leaf & Bud
Rose in the Wilderness
Magnolia Blossom
Swedish honey comb
Sister Blanket
Cross & diamonds
Rose &   "
Linen ware
Ladies Fansey
Wheeles of time

---

[3]Laura Allen made some notations next to the list of drafts. In particular she noted the 5 harness drafts "Cross & diamonds" (#43 in the draft book) and "Rose & diamonds" (#184 & 185 in the draft book).

Kingston R I 5th mo 17th 1912

I send you to days Mail

The drafts Those on Past Board

Is to Bulkey to Send By mail

So I send The old original drafts
No hurry about Returning Them

Those on new paper is from
        Virginia

Ellen hause[4]

Syngers Glen Va

E D Chapman
Clarks falls Conn Box 31
has many Drafts and would

Like to Correspond with you
he has the most of mine
My grand Farthers and mothers

Drafts wer burned to get them
Out of the way

    W h h Rose Box 63

        27th
Kingston R I 11th mo 1912[5]

The Top I Sent you

Some Time ago was The

Wisconsin Beauty

Which is just Like

Lady Washingtons
Delight We are Both Well
hope you and yours are
the same
      W h h Rose

---

[4]This letter has the most eccentric use of capitals in all of the correspondence. Laura Allen did indeed go on to correspond with Ellen Hause and E.D. Chapman. Several of their drafts are in the Allen draft collections.

[5]This is the last letter and was written in ink. A note above the letter, written in pencil by Laura Allen, reads: "Note — These letters are from the Famous "Weaver Rose" of R.I. Signed — L.M. Allen. Judging from the date of the letter, November 27, 1912, the personal references, the only ones in the whole correspondence, possibly resulted from Mrs. Allen's visit to the Roses the previous September. This visit left a deep impression on Elsie. It was from this singular occasion that Elsie's correspondence took wing.

Elsie Rose, a small, thin woman, was definitely the more educated of the two. She was Weaver Rose's partner for life in business and reclusive existence; her devotion to him was complete. It was she who carried on a correspondence with Laura Allen from 1912 to 1925. Her letters describe their hard working lives. Elsie was the housekeeper, fellow weaver, stockkeeper, gardener, and family scribe. It is thought that the finer weaving was hers. We know from a letter of July 9, 1916, that at the age of 79 she was still weaving and teaching the craft. She used one of the looms in the loft.

The words of her letters are to a great degree spelled phonetically; the handwriting is better than average, although it varies greatly — perhaps because her vision gave a certain amount of trouble. Punctuation was not important to Elsie; she never used it. Since the greater part of her correspondence was written after Weaver Rose's death, the loneliness is haunting, but the daily life which is portrayed is well worth the telling.

This correspondence, thirty-six letters, was written to Laura Allen in Rochester, New York, over a period of thirteen years. At least once a visitor in the Rose home, Mrs. Allen actively exchanged weaving information with Weaver Rose. With Elsie she discussed not only weaving but patchwork, basketry, roses, animals, and family matters. It was Laura Allen who took photographs of the Rose livestock and pets. She also was a basketmaker of note, and sent Elsie some baskets which were much admired.

The letters are reproduced as written, the number of words to the line exact. Spelling and punctuation are also exact. The original writing is in longhand. Where words cannot be deciphered, dots are inserted. The letters were all written on the same lined paper as Weaver Rose's, and also were folded to five inches wide by six inches tall.

Kingston R I Jan 8th 1913

To thee[1] thee best of all my firends a few days ago I went to Wickford
thre simple lines to thee I send I called to one place saw an aged
I think of thee Laurie in York with Lady 87 in bed helpless was
they little Stork taken sick last Feb her face was
The Book came to hand all so beautiful so placid was pleased
rite and I presume the to see me was willing and ready to
Baskets are in the ofice all to die did not want to live to be a burden
right many thanks for all She gave me a very affectionate farewell
you will hear from me again hoped we would meet above her
Wm is not very well Daughter has the whole care of her
I will be so pleased with She is very frail twice operated on
the baskets you are so very kind for a cancer Then I pased on to an
wate not for an invitation come other place saw an old lady
when ever you can I can meet 90 her hair was white as snow her eyes
you if I know when you were all faded she looked very nice
will be welcome to a cup of tea was sit by the window in the sun I can
and a jonny[2] I think we will have never forget the look as I entered the
a nice time I have been knitting room as she raised hr eyes she spoke
mittens To morrow I go South of Sister mind was very clear her
will see my firend when I saw Daughters hav all gone before her
her she had a bad cold pinkie[3] is carred for be Strangers how
is well like wise Pulaski and much we have to be thankfull for
Tyreus[4] I hope thee and and thine I well now close be wishing you a happy
are well this beautifull new year and . . . year yours with love
how many never see its dawn

EMB Rose [76 years old]

---

[1]Thee and thy are typical Quaker pronouns in speech and writing, and are found throughout Elsie's correspondence.
[2]Jonny or Jonneycake is made of cornmeal, especially popular in Colonial times. Since wheat was not produced in Rhode Island, corn would have proved a less expensive flour to use.
[3]Pinkie Rose, Elsie's horse, was her means of transportation, and was used for riding or pulling a carriage.
[4]Tyreus and Pulaski were some of the Rose dogs.

Excerpts from a letter dated Kingston R I Apr 15 1913

To my friend Laurie
. . . I am going to send you
a pece of Wm work I intended
for Easter it is not nice
it will make a little kiver
for the babe[5] it was not made
for a kiver do as you like
with it you come any time you
can stay long enog to rest
and make you a spread to take
back with you. . . .
    Wm is quite well has had several
very sick spells It makes it very
hard for me. . . .
we are on the post road the Stag used to
run from Kingston to Providence
every day Wm goes to Prov ofen
but not in that maner When not well
enough to go I go myself. . . .
since I can remmember my Mother took
a flece of wool Carded it into rowls and
spun it into yarn and then wove a
piece of broad cloth had it fuled
and colored brown Wm is a feeble
man I think more then most people
think. . . .
    Yours truly
        E M B Rose

Kiss the Babe for me the dear
little one how is the dye pot

---

[5]This and other mentions of a baby probably refer to Mrs. Allen's sister's child.

Kingston R I Aug 17 1913

My Dear firend
        Your dog came
Yesterday he is beautifull I was
pleased. . . .
. . . .Mrs H has
lost her dog Distemper don't
waite fr an invitation and stay
as long as you can I will try to
make it pleasent and have a
nice time We are as well as
usual Wm has all the weaving
he can do I go out Fridas
am buisy all the time
I am cleaning my dining
room How is th little Sister
and Babe I will want the
pictures of the stock you take
them so nice. . . .
        Yors with much Love
        E M B Rose

Wm is weaving a Mount vernon
bed Spread one bright blue one
bright pink one purple
they are very pretty I think
you will say wat a strange
letter
. . . .you know I am old and
cannot write very well I have
just had in 4 pounds of tea the
same brand I had when you
were here plenty of cream
and Jonecakes come and we
will have a nice time. . .
your letters are a great comfrt
to me I am so lonely dear firend

November 10th[6]
My Dear Brother has
pafsed a way it is very
hard too bear I am all alone
I must try to be . . . .
think of me some times
        E M B Rose

Kingston R I Nov 23 1913

Dear Firend
It is with a sad hart that I write thee once more
I am all alone I was lone with him when
he passed away and I laid him out It was
a solemn time he died in my arms was taken
ten in the morning died the next morn
ing after 3 . . . .
Mr and Mrs Holand have
ben here to day to pass thanks
giving
        Yours Truly
        E M B   Rose

---

[6]Weaver Rose died November 9, 1913

"A Rhode Island Weaver". Elsie Rose, 1924. This photo appeared on the front cover of Universal Windings, *volume 7, number 1, October, 1924. Courtesy of the Little Rest Archives, Kingston Free Library.*

Kingston R I Jan 25 1914

My Dear Friend
    Yours received sorry to
hear you are not well
My health is very good
    I am taking care of 8
head of stock be sides Pinkie
Rose It has ben very cold
hre some people lost all of
their sence You remember
ny Dear English Shepherd Dog
well he has passed a way
was poisoned was a great
guard I miss him
I have another Scoth Collie
female They may take her
next
I have found a bow n arrow[7]
and will return yours

. . . .

Mrs. T[8] said her work was muc
h nicer than Wms pled very
hard for the drafts
I am going to get them together

an lock them up
It was a great disapointmen
t to Brother as well as my
self we had laid meny plans
for your coming will be so
glad to see you any time
I am staying all alone with
my dogs
    It is sad to get up
in the morning to find
his seat vacant
Poor Dear Roy[9] hed got all
his yarns for the winters work
Oh if I could see one na while
it would be such a comfort
I beleve the good Farther is
taking care of me tears fall
as I write Friends have
ben very kind in sending
letters of sympathy which is
some comfort I read them
over n over am always so
glad to hear from you

---

[7]Refers to a weaving pattern.
[8]Mrs. "T" refes to Mrs. Arnold Talbot, the same woman mentioned in other letters. She gained Elsie's animosity, probably because she claimed "her work nicer than Wms."
[9]The "Roy" referred to was an orphan taken in by Elsie's father until manhood. This note suggests he may have worked in the general store or just ordered Weaver Rose's yarns.

Kingston R I Oct 6th 1914

Dear Firend
　　　　Hope thee will excuse
me this time I am well and
buisy think of thee every day
hope thee are well by this time
. . .It is very dry every thing
is parched up
How I wish I could see thee
this eve ning my Dogs are
fast asleep I milk two Cows
night and morning
. . . .[10]
　　　　I am
prepairing for the Cold
Winter have set up the heater[11]
have a kind firend that finds me
plenty of wood to burn. . . .
　　　　Ever your Friend
　　　　E M B Rose

Kingston R I mo 22
[there is no year indicated]

My dear Mrs. Allen
. . . .A regards the
PIllow tops there was no charge
for them I would like the
Indian war[12] agin when you
get the pattern that is the
only one
Mrs Arnold Talbt came here to get
drafts and looms went away as lite
as she came[13]

. . . .

Mr Chapman[14] has not come
yet

. . . .

As I sit writing mdogs are
by my side
　　　　hope you will have
a nice Cristmas
　　　　Truly yours
　　　　E M B Rose

---

[10]In this letter one line difficult to read mentions that she needs a pair of glasses to "see in".
[11]There was no central heating except for the central fireplace. In the weaving ell there was no heat at all.
[12]"Indian War" is probably draft #57.
[13]Mrs. Arnold Talb[o]t was most likely the Mrs T referred to in Elsie's letter of January 25, 1914. Elsie did not like her then, and certainly did not change her mind. Due to the date of the first letter, and to the 'Cristmas' reference further down, it would seem probable that this letter could be dated December 22, 1914.
[14]Mr. Chapman must refer to E.D. Chapman of Clarks Falls, Connecticut, to whom WHHR referred in his third letter.

Kingston R I Aug 21 1914

My Dear Friend

I received you letter contain
ing the sad news do you
have the Doc to sett your
hip if so you will never keep
It in place by all means
have Bonesetter Sweet
I suppose there is one in
every place we have one
in Wakefield I wish
you were with me
Howw long has It beenout
I have k[n]own of such cures

The Ds do not like the
Sweets they have trid
to put them down from
Doc trine[15]

I am well I wish you
wer the same
. . . .

My Brother would
Have ben a cripple but
for Dr. Sweet

A lady came here with her
ankle out Sweet came here
and set it now he ses get
up and walk and she did
all rite pleas excuse an
old lady for giving advice
I have kown so much of them
and feel so much
for thee dear Firend[16]
E M B R

---

[15]The Doctors do not like the Sweets they have tried to put them down from Doctoring [sic].
This sounds like the old argument about M.D.s and chiropractors.
[16]And again in her letter of March 15, 1917, ". . . We now have a D R In the place I called him
once to my Dog he seems very nice has a very young wife. . . ."

Kingston R I Novem 15 1914[17]

Dear firend
         One year last monday
my Dear Brother was laid away
for ever from my sight he now
out in the cold wind and rain
How I wish you could be here
You must not work so hard take a
rest and thee will be stronger
I am well wish you were as well
Mrs. H and Husband have ben
sick with a cold
If I do not write I think
of thee as the wind passes
over me as do the opening
flowers.

It is all in thinkin I am
just a poor old lady
Try some time to come
please write often as thee has
time your letters are very

cheering my glasses do not
stay on I cant see very well
I will be all alone This cold
winter I have two cows and
one a two year and Pinky
to look after two dogs
and 4 little pups they are
very cunning wish you were
here to take their pictures
I could give you jonny cake
a cup of tea
I must close with love to
you and all of yours
                    Elsie

please write often
May every day thou present to see
be better than the past
I wis I new how to make baskets
like you do It would be very
pleasant these winter evenings

---

[17]This letter, written on the first anniversary of WHHR's death, November 9, 1913, is one of few signed by her first name. In spite of the pathos of it, there is still evident an affirmation of life.

Kingston R I Apr 26 1914

The beautiful S[p]ring time
has dawned upon us once more
soon the flowers will come
fourth once more to pleas us
what is the name of your Roses[18]
Wm was very fond of flowers
used to find pretty wild
flowers. . . .

Slocum R I may 13 1915

Dear Firend
          Just a few lines
this time I am well and
quite bisy this is buisnes
Roses is the theme Of It
Is not too late and thee
can send me some and
the bill the Yellow Dorthy
Perkins American Beauty
red
White American Beauty
His mjisty
Baron de Ronstetten
Conrad ferdinand Myer
I hope thou art well
do not work to hard
Good Bye and good
luck
          from old Rosie
please send Slocum R I
RFD

---

[18]Flowers, especially roses, were an important part of Elsie's life. WHHR's preference for wild
flowers is noted in a letter of April 26, 1914.

Slocum R I Aug 1915

My Dear Laura

yours came to hand in due time
am very sory to hear of thy poor
health I think if thee could
be here the air is so good thee
would soon be better It would
cheer my poor old aking heart to
see the once more I am all alone
I received the card and many
thanks It was so prety I almst
wanted to send for some then
It would trouled to mch
Mrs. Holland Is quite well
comes as often a chenc permits
I am well and do all my work
I milk two cows take care of Pinke
Rose 30 hens and 6 dogs and
my garden which keeps me quite
buisy most of the time
had I the wings of a dove I would
quickly fly to thee bt alas It
canot be will write as often as I can
I am spending this sundy evening
inconversing with thee whch Is
a great pleasure to me hope thee
will write often I have many
callers from difrent parts of the
country allmost every one Is
kind to me I keep the tray
on the front room table to receive
my cards It is very much

admired by many people
that call would that I had the
art of making such Is not this
war terrible
It has been raining hard all day
the Summer has been very dry
so but little hay has been cut
have not one quarter what I
had last year Potatoes are
rotting very badly how is your
garden Thoes tomatoes were very
nice of which seed thee sent
but I lost mice is distrutive
you do not have any in a new
house like yours I think thee
will be tired of my rambling
note I shall anhsious to
hear how you are please write
often as you feel able
Are thee able to go to Church
Wish you could have a good old
fashion joney cake and a cup
of tea with me how pleasent
It would seem

It nine oclock and my dogs
have all gone to sleep and I
must say good bye hoping
hear from thee soon
Truly thy Firend
        E M B Rose

Slocum R.I. Aug.   19 15

My Dear Laura

Yours came to hand in due time
I am very sorry to hear of thy poor
health. I think if thee could
be here the air is so good thee
would soon be better. It would
cheer my poor old aking heart to
see thee once more. I am all alone

It is nine oclock and my dogs
have all gone to sleep and I
must say good bye hoping
hear from thee soon

Truly thy Friend

E. M. R. Rose

Excerpts from a letter written by Elsie Rose to Laura Allen, July 9, 1916.

July 9th 1916

Dear Firend
Yours received pleased
to hear from thee
I fear thy health is no better
give up all business and rest thy
dear Body and mind
had I the wings of a dove I
would fly to the for a little
While then return to the place
where I was Born If thee
could come and stay with
me you could [take Pinky go in saddle or carriage]
and go down to see Mrs
H every morning for your health
you would be welcome and
I would be pleased to have
Thee come I am all allone
the good Farther has given
me health and strength
which is a great blessing
. . . .

We are having a tempist to
day
I could give
thee corn cakes and tea and
eggs and a little something
beside my garden   Is looking
nice I work it all my self
take care of my stock and
weave a little so you see I am
quite buisy. . . .
I have two dogs and 3 pups
I am going to lern a young
lady to weave
. . . .
                    Sincerely Yours
                    Elsie

Kingston R I Dec 17th 1916   Kingston R I March the 15th 1917

Dear Firend do not think
I have forgoten thee such is
not the case I am buisy. . . .
. . .Have just had a
cold hard snow storm
I had my paths to make
to get to Pinky Rose
and my cow I have 4 dogs
I have just received a pack
age from N Y . . .not to be
opened until Chrismas
It is hard to wait so long
Thee must enjoy thy
auto rides well pinky
will do for me what is
the price of eggs 60 cents
here s[c]arce at that
Mrs Holland is quite
well I had a thanksgivin
lunch come in
Roast Chicken apple pie
crambry sauce pumpkin pie
and other things had a
sweater given me for
Exmas people are very
kind to me . . .
. . .yours with much
love Truly yours   Elsie

My Dear Firend Laura

I would like to see you and convers
with the as that cannot be I will
try the pen the next best way
Glad you feel al little Beter I wish
you were well and strong like me
We have had a cold hard winter
I have been able to make my paths
to the barn go up the ladder
throw down hay and milk and
get my breakfast I am so glad
Spring here once more the Birds
will soon begin to sing and
and the flowers bloom It
will be bautifull I wish thee could
come we would have a nice time
your stay was so short before
. . . .
we are on the post road the Stage
Coch use to run twice a day from
Kingston to Providence some
time after The cars wer put
through You found no trouble
to find the place
we always treat people with
respect that call to the place
. . .We now
have a DR In the place
I called hime once to my
Dog he seems very nice has
a very young wife my pen and
ink are both very poor the
                writer the
same please overlook It all
           Yours with much love
                E M B R

Kingston R I Oct 28 1917[19]

Dear Friend
        It has been along
time since I received your
Letter have been very buisy
have almost got my garden
I had some squashes and
a nice lot of beans Have
quite amply for winter
wish thee could be here to help
me eat them we could have some
Chicken and sqash pie

                November 20ond 1917

Dear Firend Yours received
I dont think there has been
a day but what I have
thought of thee I would say
I write this eve when that
time comes I am tired and sleepy
and cant see very well
I hope thee will over look the
neglect of so dear a Firend I am
very sorry to hear of thy misfotune
Truly thee must suffer very
much Thee must take a long
rest rest will do thee more
good than money I supose
I will never see thee again In
this life Good bye very
There Is a better land I am
all alone with my Dogs 7 in
number the old dog had
8 pups sold 4 I have one

Cow and Pinky Rose 20 hens
It is very cold here a very
backward season I have not
seen a soldier I dont go out
and they dont come this way
the times are terrble we are
just on the edge of It no Sugar
to be had I was geting in my
winter Stores and had took
2 Dollars worth and was going
to get mor there was none
to be had I dved with
Mrs Holland fo her quinces
                Truly Yours Anty Rose

They hav given m 4 bshels
of potatoes turnips carrots onions
pars nips beets and beans
they are true firends and
a nice pair of shoes
I have had a present from
Providence R I a very nice
cape coat and two wrappers
I have no reason to complain
allmost every one Is kind
to me I wish thee could be with
me to cheer me on my way
my journey Is allmost over
I took Mrs H out to get her
suply o grocries She steped very
spry and quick she Is so very
kind to me hope she well be blest
In the better land

---

[19]This letter and the following one, written in pencil, were sent together.

· 35 ·

[November, 1918][20]

My Dear Firend
                I will this
day thy kind letter of
so long a go dont think I have
forgoten the[e] I hope this cor
rpondence so . . . silent a
year I have had the grip
and since have been neither
sick or well hope thee has
escaped and in good hea
lth
                the war is over there Is no
men that Is fit to work
even to plant a garden
I suppose yours Is look
ing vry fine and the roses in
full bloom How I wish
I could see thee It would
cheer this poor old heart
but alafs It cannot be as
I cannot go to the[e] and the[e]
cannot come to me you are
young I am old I cannot
forget the pleasant time
we had with thee though
short every thing has
changed since then Mrs
Holland has split the bone
and broke the tendon on her
thimble finger quite well
otherwise

They are two good People
It is very dry here the grapes
drying we need rain so badly
well I have five dogs to keep
me company 3 Cats how Is
that little girl do you weave
now I do a little can Thee
get the flat shoe lacings
in your place if so please
send me a bunch and the
price cannot get them here
the price of every thing Is
going higher and Higher here
This country will never be the same
again the flowers of thee
land have been taken aw
ay never to return I had none
to go but felt for others
I hope this will find you all
well there has been a great
deal of sicknefs here and
deaths a woman 92 a. . . .
of 62 lived many days with
out any nourishment at all
when a boy came to live with
my farthr a poor little orphn
Roy stayd untill manhood
and then went out to work
please write me all about
your sicknes now I must
close with love
                Yours Truly
                Rose

---

[20]This letter had no date, but because she mentions the war being over and the amount of sick-
ness, the year was probably 1918, the year of the Armistice.

[December 25, 1924]

Dear Friend
                    I take my pen
once more to see what it
. . . say although silent yet
seldom out of mind
I have had my paper out
a number of times to write
something would hender
I am In the old House
all alone with my dogs
and cats I have just lost
my dog that was my door
keeper I miss him he would
hee would tel me when any one
was at the door I cant hear
very quick I am old and feeble
Thee does not realize how chering
It is to have a letter from a
friend It is very cold and
dreary Exmas day no one will
be in so I will spend the time
in writing to a Dear friend
had it been pleasant Mrs
Holland would have been
with me She has lost her
dear husband her health is
very poor she comes when
ever she can I am greatly
blest the good Lord has
given me many good friends
I have been been wel remembered
this Chrismas day and I
wish Thee a happi one I have
a Friend In new York that
sends me th new York times

how are thee in stile has thee
boberd thy hair it gives
the hair workers buisness
a good head of hair is a greet
ornement I think the Talbo
ts have rather failed a man came
that was interested in them
wanted borrow all the [d]
rafts would be responsible
for them but I said no
he said If some one would
come in and [copy] them
he thought the drafts shoul
d not [put] by and lost
I will not let them go out
of the house[21] Mr Brigs
. . . nephew came and
copied them Mr Brigs is
a weaver and is teaching
this nephew to weave

I am sending a little paper
that you may see my old
face when I am no mor
at the same time I
send this do not wate
for me to write a letter
would be so cheering
                    Truly Your friend
                    Elsie M B Rose

---

[21]EMBR seemed pleased that the Talbots had given up on trying to obtain the drafts, but she let another weaver, not previously mentioned, copy them.

Slocum R I April 27 1925

My Dear Friend
I am still here in the
old house all alone have
a bad cold I dont often
have a cold not like this
Tel m[e] all about your arm
you can have the papers[22]
when it is a little warmer
so I can get up stairs
I have an old poem I am
going to get copied the lines . . .
What maters no lifes darkest day
When God has wiped all tears away
It was sung for Dr Woods Servis
in Newport he I[s] a Friend
of mine This Is a beautiful
Aprill Day I now tel me
all about your arm was It
broken I would like to take
a cup of tea with thee
it would be good
        Adieu
      From yor Firend

Slocum R I

June 24 1925
My Dear Firend A few lines
to tel the package Starts
with this note you nede
not return them
I hope you are beter so you can
enjoy life I as glad to
k[n]ow you not alone and
have your Husband with
you Mr Holland[23] is not
well Bye and B She will
be with me the warm days
was almost to much for me
      Loving yours
      E M B R

Friday morning

You will say it is an
old womans work
      Dear Firend
        adieu

---

[22]This must refer to the weaving drafts.
[23]Mrs. Holland is meant here, as Mr. Holland was dead.

July 25

My Dear Friend
        Just a line to
tel I am well many thanks
for what you sent me something
that is always handy[24]
This is reel dog days
I am glad you enjoy
the papers
and good bye and good
luck to the[e] May
Gods Blessing . . . upon thee
            Yours with love
                Elsie

[This was the last letter. Elsie died on May 14 of 1926.]

---

[24]Probably Mrs. Allen had received the drafts and sent some money for them.

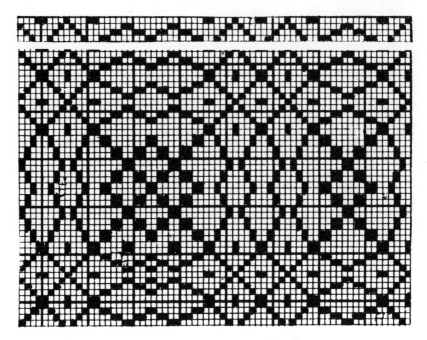

Figure 1. Pattern #154. "No Name". Profile or block draft.

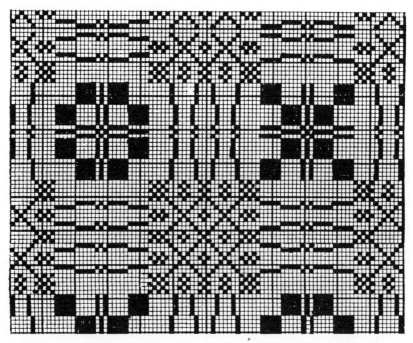

Figure 2. "Flowers of Canaan", a pattern Weaver Rose used to weave a waistcoat fabric for "a Boston gentleman." Profile or block draft.

·WEAVER ROSE PATTERNS·

The Draft Book Of
William Henry Harrison Rose

"He has about 100 patterns, he says, but never originated any. They are mostly on cardboard, for convenience, but some of them remain in the old papers, yellowed with age, on which they have come down to him through the last 80 years."

The Providence Journal
October 8, 1905

"Dear Miss Van Cleve,
. . . I am enclosing a partial list of some of Weaver Rose. Many of them were on boards. Sometimes a name and date. The short way of writing drafts I managed easily, all but those like the one I enclose "Seven Stars". I found many drafts started at the left to thread, some at the right, and some in the middle. I copied the spelling. . . . Also a fringe which I will send as soon as I can make a description.

As always sincerely,
Emily Beals
June 11, [1937]

My working drafts for compiling this book were copies which Dr. Young gave me of those in the Laura Allen collection. The Allen collection, which consists of eight bound scrapbooks, is housed in the American Textile Museum in North Andover, Massachusetts. Volume VI contains the Weaver Rose collection. The copies of some 50 Rose drafts which Mrs. Beals refers to in her letter above agree with the ones in the Allen scrapbook, so I feel confident that they are as Weaver Rose originally drew them.

In compiling the Rose drafts, Mrs. Allen preserved the original titles with their eccentric spellings, Weaver Rose's comments on the drafts, and also their origins as noted by him. She also made some effort to organize and annotate them. The additional comments in the headings to the drafts are hers; they describe the condition in which she found the original (often written on scraps of dated newspapers which indicate when Weaver Rose copied them), and in some cases cross-reference the drafts with the collection published later by Mary Atwater. The drafts in the Allen collection are not numbered consistently; for the reader's convenience, I have numbered them consecutively.

In reproducing the drafts for this book, obviously careless errors that seem to have happened in the process of being copied have been corrected. Other errors and anomalies are corrected in the footnotes, which were prepared by Carol Strickler.

As a weaver, I have found the "no name" drafts interesting and quite striking. Since some of these were noted as being "used a lot", perhaps Weaver Rose left them nameless because they were his favorites.

Figure 1 is "No Name #154", an overshot pattern. I've shown the draft here in profile (each square representing two threads) to demonstrate the interesting pattern, circles within circles, diamonds within diamonds. I've woven it in blue and white, which is quite striking, and also in two close shades of pink, which gives a brocade effect that is very handsome and not too busy. Figure 2 is a profile drawdown of the pattern of the waistcoat material which Weaver Rose wove in scarlet cotton and wool "for a Boston gentleman."

A number of different notation styles not familiar to contemporary weavers can be found among the drafts. A brief explanation of them, and suggestions for translating them into more easily useable form, have been prepared by Carol Strickler. Following the draft book is an appendix of computer-produced drawdowns of most of the drafts, also prepared by Carol Strickler.

Drafting Notations Explained
by Carol Strickler

Several different drafting "shorthand" conventions were used to write these drafts. Some of the threadings read left to right, some read right to left, and some read either way. All of them appear to be thread-by-thread drafts, *not* block or profile drafts.

The most familiar method of notation to today's weaver is one we can call the "modern" convention. The threading used here as an example is one invented just for this purpose, and is not one of the Rose drafts.

Modern

In this method, each horizontal row represents one shaft or harness of the loom, with the lowest or #1 shaft being the closest to the weaver. The numbers in the draft are shaft numbers, reinforcing the horizontal row indication. Each vertical row represents one warp thread. The draft could be read (and threaded) from either direction. Weaver Rose notebook drafts written in the "modern" form include #41, #46, #47, #96 and #138.

A second method of writing used here is a form we can call "condensed". In this form, the horizontal rows still represent the shafts or harnesses of the loom, but the vertical rows stand for groups of threads rather than individual threads. The numbers in "condensed" indicate the order of the threads (*not* the shafts on which they are threaded) and the number of threads in the block. Therefore a 1 on the lowest row with a 6 directly above it on the second row means "thread 6 threads on shafts 1 and 2 alternately (block 1), beginning on shaft 1 and ending on shaft 2, thusly: 1,2,1,2,1,2."

It should be mentioned here that apparently many of the old weavers wrote drafts as though shaft 1 or the lowest shaft on their draft were the *farthest* from the weaver.

In the "condensed #1" form, only the beginning and ending thread of each block is indicated. The example given here is a "condensed #1" version of the same threading as the "modern" given above. In this example, because there is a 1 at both ends, the draft could be read either left to right or right to left. "Chariot Wheels and Church Windows #3" (draft #33) and "Washington's Delight" (#103) are among the Weaver Rose drafts using this form.

Condensed #1

```
  6 6   2   2   6 6        6
  1 1             1 1
6 6     2   2       6 6
1     1 1 1 1 1 1     1 1
```

In the "condensed #2" form, *all* threads are numbered (instead of just the first and last), but their position on the horizontal rows still indicates the shaft numbers. The example given is the same threading as the previous ones, but written in "condensed #2" form. Note that since the threading needs to begin with a "thread number 1", this example reads from left to right. "Fig Leaf or Barren Tree" (draft #68) and "Rose in the Wilderness" (draft #189) are among the Weaver Rose drafts written in "condensed #2" form. (Note that #68 reads left to right and #189 reads right to left.)

Condensed #2

```
    2 4 6 2 4 6   2   2   2 4 5 2 4 6            2 4 6
  1 3 5 1 3 5                1 3 5 1 3 5
2 4 6 2 4 6          2   2   2       2 4 6 2 4 6
1 3 5        1 3 5 1 1 1 1 1 1 3 5        1 3 5 1 3 5
```

The form that we might call "condensed #3" is a blend of the two previous condensed forms. Some of the blocks are indicated by every thread being numbered; other blocks are shown by just beginning and ending figures. Somewhere in the draft there is at least one block enumerated in detail to provide a clue to direction of reading and threading. Note that both "condensed #3" examples given read left to right and are versions of the same draft given above. The majority of the overshot drafts in the Weaver Rose notebook use the "condensed #3" form of shorthand.

Condensed #3

6 6		1	1		1 5 6		6
1 1					1 1		
6 6	2		1 1			6 6	
1	1 1 3 2 2 2 2 2					1 1	

or

	6 6	2	2	6 6		2 4 6	
	1 1			1 1			
2 4 6 6		2	2	2		6 6	
1 3 5		1 1 1 1 1 1 1				1 1 3 5	

A third major category of drafts might be called "stacked". It closely resembles "condensed #1" in form, but is numbered differently. In "stacked", the horizontal rows represent shafts of the loom, and the positions of the numbers represents which shafts the threads are threaded on. The different is that in "stacked", the numbers indicate how many threads are entered on *each* shaft within the block. It does *not* tell on which shaft the block begins or ends. Therefore, a 3 on the first row with a 3 immediately above it on the second row indicates that the block is 6 threads on shafts 1 and 2 alternately, but it could be either 1,2,1,2,1,2, or 2,1,2,1,2,1. The example given is the same draft as the previous ones, written in "stacked" form. Drafts in the Weaver Rose notebook which use "stacked" shorthand include "Fox Trail" (#72) and "Magnolia Blossom" (#113). Note that there is no starting or ending indicated on these drafts, so they could read in either direction.

Stacked

3 3		1	1		3 3		3
3 3					3 3		
3 3		1	1	1	3 3		
3	3				3	3 3	

Another draft shorthand which is sometimes used could be called "ones". It uses a 1 to represent each thread, and can be either like the "modern" draft where each thread has its own vertical column, or like "condensed #2" where each vertical column shows a *pair* of threads. The "ones" example given here is the latter form. A few "ones" drafts appear in the Weaver Rose notebook, including #43 (a spot Bronson, "modern" form), and #108 (an M's & O's, "condensed #2" form).

Ones

```
        1 1 1 1 1 1   1  1   1 1 1 1 1 1                    1 1 1
    1 1 1 1 1 1                           1 1 1 1 1 1
1 1 1 1 1 1                 1    1    1              1 1 1 1 1 1
1 1 1              1 1 1 1 1 1 1 1 1 1 1              1 1 1 1 1 1
```

Overshot Conventions

The modern ways of drafting overshot weave usually place the four blocks on four adjacent pairs of shafts: 1-2, 2-3, 3-4, and 1-4. The threading is written in such a way that odd-numbered shafts alternate with even-numbered shafts throughout. This means that odds (1-3) vs. evens (2-4) will plain weave or tabby for the ground weave. But early weavers, especially in the South, often used a different form, possibly because it gave them a better shed on the roller- or horse-suspended shafts of their counterbalanced looms. In this version of overshot (which we'll call "historical"), the four blocks are written on 1-3, 2-3, 2-4, and 1-4. This places the tabbies on 1-2 vs. 3-4. The example used above is shown rewritten in "historical" form in two different drafting shorthands ("modern" and "condensed #1").

Historical Form (Modern Drafting)

```
                                                    ★         ★
            4  4  4  4  4  4     4     4     4  4  4  4  4  4 |          |         4  4  4
    3  3  3  3  3  3              3     3     3               |3  3  3  |3  3  3
        2  2  2  2  2  2                        2  2  2        |2  2  2  |
    1  1  1              1  1  1  1  1  1  1  1  1  1  1        |         |1  1  1  1  1  1
```

Historical Form (Condensed #1 Drafting)

```
        6 6   2   2   6 6      6
    6 6       2   2   2      1
    1 1               1 6 6
    1     1 1 1 1 1 1 1     1 1
```

Note that in converting a standard (1-2, 2-3, 3-4, 1-4) draft into a "historical" one, it is very easy to write blocks mistakenly inverted, so that the exact tabby order is broken (indicated by the stars marking places where two adjacent warp threads will work together in the otherwise plain weave sheds). The problem would be corrected in the example by inverting the bracketed block. This was a common drafting error which shows up in many of the surviving nineteenth century coverlets.

Among the many Weaver Rose drafts written in "historical" form are "The American Beauty" (#10, written in "condensed #2" and reading left to right), "The Arrow From N.C." (#11, written in "stacked" and reading either way), and "Chariot Wheels of South Carolina" (#36, written in "condensed #3 and reading right to left).

When an overshot threading based on small repeats of alternating opposite blocks is written in "historical" form, it very much resembles an M's & O's" weave threading. A good example of this is Weaver Rose draft #22, "Buckens and Owels". It is recorded as a "small M's & O's", but is virtually identical to Atwater's small overshot draft #3, "Turkey Foot", when treadled as overshot.

Most of the Weaver Rose drafts are overshot weave. Some are 4-block (6-shaft) summer & winter weave. Some are 2-block (4-shaft) M's & O's weave. Most of the rest are 3-block (4-shaft) spot Bronson, also called Barley Corn.

1.
Bits found among the other drafts.

```
1  5                    4    4        4   4        4   4          4
  2      2                3        3   3        3   3          3
      5 3                      2 2        2 2        2 2
2   4  5                    1   1 1    1   1 1    1   1 1
```

Tread.
1-2
1-3
3-4
1-4
1-2
2-3
3-4
1-4
1-3
3-4
1-4
1-2
1-4
3-4
1-3
1-4

2.

```
1  5                    4    4 4    4    4    4
  2                       3     3     3
      6 7                   2     2     2
4 4      8                1 1 1 1 1   1 1 1   1
```

Tread.
1-4
1-3
1-4
2-4
1-2
1-4
1-3
1-4
2-4
1-2
1-4
1-3

3.

```
1    5                  4    4    4    4    4    4
  3                       3     3     3
         7                  2 2   2 2   2 2
2  4    8                 1 1   1 1   1   1 1   1
```

Tread.
1-4
1-3
1-4
2-4
1-2
2-4
1-4
1-3
1-4
2-4
1-2

1, 2, 3. The first two read right to left, the last one left to right. The right-hand portion of each of these drafts seems to be someone's interpretation of the bits on the left which don't make obvious sense.

4.

Scraps among other drafts.

```
2        1   3      2              2 4      2 4
   1 3       1 3       1 3 1   3       1   3    1   3 2 4
   2 4       2 4       2 4 2         2        2
1   3      2       1   3         1 3       1 3       1 3
```

Tread.
1-2
2-3
3-4
1-4
3-4
2-3
1-2
1-4
1-2
2-3
3-4

Corrected

```
4        4   4      4              4   4      4           4   4
   3   3       3   3       3   3       3   3       3   3       3
   2   2       2       2   2       2   2       2   2         2
1   1       1       1   1       1       1   1       1
```

5.

```
2          4 2        3 1   2        2                          5 3 1
3 1   2      5 3 1 4 2          3 1   2    3 1   2      4   2
    3 1   2        3 1   4 2            3 1   2    3 1   2 5   3 1   4   2
       3 1              5 3   1 4 2        3 1          3 1        5   3   1   4 2
```

6.

```
   5 3 1   5 3 1
4 2      1          4 2   4 2 3 1
5 3 1        2   4 2 5 3 1          4 2
    4 2              5 3 1
```

7.

```
4 2 4 2 4 2 4 2 4 2 4 2 4 2
   3 1      3 1      3 1

3 1      3 1      3 1      3 1
```

8.

```
1          1        1   1 3 5            1 3                  1 3 5
   1 1 1   1 3 1 1   1        1 3 5 1 3 1 3    1 3 1 3 1 3 5      1 3
   4          4              2 4          2 4
6 6    4 6 2 4   6 6 2 2 4 6 2 4 6    2 4 2 4 2 4    2 4 6 2 4 6 2 4
```

---

4. Left to right, standard, condensed #2. The final (right) 2 and 4 should be on the top line. The "corrected" version still has several errors. The pattern is a two-block overshot similar to Rose #110 and related to Atwater #121-#125, a Monk's Belt or Window Sash pattern.

5. Right to left, standard, condensed #2. A very broken diagonal pattern.

6. Right to left, historical, condensed #2. A small overshot, similar to Atwater #4.

7. Right to left, standard, condensed #2. A simple two-block pattern that could be treated as two-block spot Bronson or huck.

8. Left to right, historical, condensed #3. Same as Rose #133. This is a small overshot similar to Atwater #30 and #32, Sweet Briar Beauty and The Cleveland Web.

9.

"Alabama Beauty". *On ad for coffee. A duplicate on dirty brown paper.*

```
1   1        1 3      1 3        1        1 3      1 3        1        1 3      1 3        1 1   1   1   1   1   1   1 1
    1   1 3 1 3      1 3      1 3 1 3    1 3 1 3      1 3      1 3 1 3    1 3 1 3      1 3      1 3 1 3  1  1 3  1 3  1 3  1 3  1 3  1 3  1
        8 8 2 4          2 4          8 2 4          2 4          2 4 6 2 4          2 4          2 4 8    2 4  2 4  2 4  2 4  2 4  2 4  8
4         2 4 2 4      2 4 2 4 2 4      2 4 2 4      2 4 2 4          2 4 2 4      2 4 2 4      8 8  6  6  6  6  6  6 8
```

Tread
```
3-1   3-2   3-1
3-2   2-4   3-2
3-4   4-1   4-2
2-3   3-1   4-1
2-1   3-2   3-4
4-1   4-2   etc.
1-3   3-2
      3-1
      4-1
```

10.

"The American Beauty" *or* "White House".

```
2 4 6        2      2      2        2 4 6 2 4    1 3      1 3      1 3 5    1 3 5    1 3 5    1 3 5    1 3 5 1 3 5 7              1
      2 4 6 2 4  1 3  1 3  1 3 2 4 6          1 3      1 3      1 3      1 3      1 3      1 3      1 3          1 3 5 7 1 3   2 4
1 3 5 1 3 5      1      1      1    1 3 5 1 3 5                                                        2 4 6 8 2 4 6 8    2
        1 3      2 4    2 4    2 4      1 3 2 4 2 4 2 4 2 4 2 4 2 4 6 2 4 2 4 6 2 4 2 4 6 2 4 2 4 6 2 4 2 4 6 2 4 2 4 6 2 4 6    2 4   1 3
```

	Treadle	
	1-3	2-3
	2-3	2-4
	2-4	2-3
	2-3	1-3
	1-2	1-4
	1-4	1-3
	1-3	2-3
	2-3	2-4
	2-4	1-4
	1-4	3-4
	1-3	

```
1      1        1 3 5 7 1 3    1 3      1 3      1 3      1 3      1 3      1 3      1 3      1 3      1 3      1 3
    2 4   2 4 2 4 6 8        1 3      1 3      1 3      1 3      1 3      1 3      1 3      1 3      1 3      1 3
2      2    1 3 5 7 2 4 6 8    2 4      2 4      2 4      2 4      2 4      2 4      2 4      2 4      2 4      2 4
    1 3   1 3          2 4      2 4      2 4      2 4      2 4      2 4      2 4      2 4      2 4      2 4      2 4
```

11.

```
5      1  1  1      5 4  4  4  4  4  4  4 5  1  1  1      5 2  2  2  2  2  2  2  2  2  2  2
    5 2  2  2  2 5      2  2  2  2  2  2      5 2  2  2  2 5  2  2  2  2  2  2  2  2  2  2  2
5 5  1  1  1  5 5                          5 5  1  1  1  5 5 2  2  2  2  2  2  2  2  2  2
    2  2  2  2      4 2 4 2 4 2 4 2 4 2 4 2 4 2 4 2 4      2  2  2  2      2  2  2  2  2  2  2  2  2  2  2
```

---

9. Left to right, historical, condensed #3. This pattern is labelled Monk's Belt, but is really Pine Bloom overshot (also called Pine Burr, Isle of Patmos, Star of the Sea, or Seven Stars). See Atwater #26 and Rose #173.

10. Left to right, historical, condensed #3. The treadling given is twill-like. Treadled as drawn in, this is a three-table overshot distantly related to several Atwater drafts, but it is not the same as Atwater's American Beauty, which is a wheel with diamonds.

11. Reads either way. Historical, stacked. Similar to Rose #10 and #143, and to Atwater #82, The Arrow, and #48, King's Flower.

12.

"The Arrow from N.C." on a very dirty bit of cardboard.

```
1 3 1   3 1 1 3 1 1 3 1 1   3 1 1 3 1   3 1       4 2 8 4 2
        1                   1 1         1     8 4 2         8 8
8     8     8     8     8   8 4 2   4 2       3 1 3 1   3 1 1
    4 2   4 2   4 2   4 2   8       8     8 4 2 1       1       1
```

13.

"Bachelor's Fancy" on back of ad for "Castoria", 35 doses for 25 cents.
A second draft uses 6 instead of 8 and reads "Bachelors Fancey". Evidently used a great deal.

```
      2        1 3 2      1 3      1 3 8  2 4    2 4  8 2      1 3      1 3 2          1 3   8  8  8  8  8  8      1 3
   2 1 3 2            1 3 2 4 2 4 2 4 2              1 3 2 6 2 4 2 4 2      1 3 2  1 3 1 1 1 1 1 1 1 1 1 1 1 1 3 2   1 3
 2 1 3      1 3 2        1 3    1 3    8  2 4  8      1 3    1 3      1 3 2      2 4  4  4  4  4  4  2        2
 1 3          1 3 2          1 1 1 3 1 3 1 3 1 1          1 3 2
```

```
   2  1 3    1 3    2  1  1 3      1 3  1 1 3    2 4    2  1 3
   2  1 3 2 4 1 3 1 3          2  1 3 1 3 1 3 1 3
 1 3        2 4    2 4      1    1 3    1     2 4    2 4
 2  1 3          8 8 2 4 2 4 2 4 2 4 8 8              2
```

14.

"Blazing Star", #1 & #3 on dark red brown mussed paper.

```
   5 3 1  2          4 4 5 3 1 1      3  1  4 2        5 3 1  4 2        5 3 1  4 2        3 1 1
       3  1  2      3 3      2  3  1  2        5 3 1  4 2        5 3 1  4 2        3  1  2 2 1
 4 2        3  1  2  2 2    3 3 1  2      5 3 1  4 2      5 3 1  4 2      3  1  2      3 2
 5 3 1  4 2        3  1 1 1  4 2 4 4 2      5 3 1  4 2      5 3 1  4 2      5 3 1  2        4 3
```

---

12. Right to left, historical, condensed #3. Similar to Rose #211 and Atwater #82.

13. Left to right, standard, condensed #3. This pattern is different from the one Atwater calls Bachelor. It begins and ends with a wheel, so if repeated it would be a form of Double Chariot Wheel or Double Lover's Knot with Table.

14. Right to left, standard, condensed #2. This is not a Blazing Star, in which the diagonal just widens from the center. It is a Double Bow Knot, in which the diagonals flare and then taper back to a point.

15.

```
4 2 4 4 4 2              5 3 1   4 2                5 3 1   4 2
  3 3 3 1   2                5 3 1   4 2                5 3 1   4 2
    2 2   3   1   2                5 3 1   4 2                5 3 1
3 1 1 1         3   1   4 2                5 3 1   4 2
```

```
7 3      6 4 2 5 1        3   1   4 2        5 3 1   4 2          5 3 1   4 2          3   1 4   7 5 3 1   4 4 2
6 2        6 2   3   1   2        5 3 1   4 2          5 3 1   4 2          3   1   2   5 1        7 3
3   1        7 3 4 2   2        4 2   4 2          5 3 1   4 2          3   1   2        6 2        6 2
4      7 5 3 1   4 3 1        5 3 1 5 3 1          5 3 1   4 2          5 3 1   2        7 3   6 4 2 5 1 3 1
```

```
2            3 1   4 2                5 3 1   4 2                5 3 1   2
3   1   2        5 3 1   4 2                5 3 1   4 2                3   1   2
      3   1        5 3 1   4 2        5 3 1   4 2                3   1   2
          4 2        5 3 1   4 2        5 3 1   4 2          3   1
```

16.
"Block Center, Diamonds at Corners", *fairly recent.*

```
1   1   1   1     1     1     1          3 1      3 1              3 1          3 1      3 1      3 1
8 4 8 4 8 4 8 4 2 8 4 2 8 4 2 8 4 2          4 2 4 2 4 2     4 2 4 2 4 2          4 2 4 2 4 2          4 2
  1   1   1   31     31     31     3131          31      3 1 3 1 3 1     3131          31      31      3131
                          4 2 4 2          4 2          4 2 4 2          4 2 4 2
```

17.
"Block and Diamonds", *on brown paper.*

```
5 3 1 5 3 1        3 1 3 1      3 1 3 1            5 3 1 5 3 1
    6 4 2 4 2        4 2      4 2      6 4 2 6 4 2          8              8            8            8 6 4 2 8 6 4 2
      3 1 3 1          4 2        3 1 5 3 1        7 5 3 1 7 5 3 1 7 5 3 1 7 5 3 1 7 5 3 1 7 5 3 1 7 5 3 1 7 5 3 1 7 5 3 1
6 4 2        4 2 4 2      3 1      4 2 4 2          6 4 2  8            8            8            8
```

15. Right to left, standard, condensed #2. A variant of Rose #14.

16. Right to left, standard, condensed #3. Related to Rose #11 and #143, and Atwater #82, a flawed Arrow pattern.

17. Right to left, standard, condensed #2. The first (right) block of eight threads should be on the bottom two rows instead of the middle. See also Rose #46, #165 and #210. This is similar to Atwater's Single Orange Peel and Cross of Tennessee.

· 51 ·

18.
"THE BLooMING LEAF", *on a very mussed & wrinkled large piece of redish brown paper.*

```
                                                                    1 1        1 3 5 1 3 5         1 3 5
    2 4 6      2 4 6      2 4 6      2 4 6      2 4 6      2 4 6      2 4 6      2 4 6      2 2 4       2 4 6 2 4
1 3 5 1 3 5 1 3 5 1 3 5 1 3 5 1 3 5 1 3 5 1 3 5 1 3 5 1 3 5 1 3 5 1 3 5 1 3 5 1 3 5 1 3 5    1 3 1 3        1 3 1 3
2 4 6      2 4 6      2 4 6      2 4 6      2 4 6      2 4 6      2 4 6      2 4 6      2 4 6 2     2 4 2 4 6        2 4 2 4 6
```

```
1 3 5 1 3 5 1 3 5        1 3 1 3        1 3 1 3          1 3 1 3          1 3 1 3          1 3 5 1 3 5 1 3 5 1 3 5       1 3 5
2 4 6       2 4 6 2 4 6        2 4 2 4        2 4 2 4        2 4 2 4        2 4 2 4        2 4 6 2 4 6        2 4 6        2 4 2 4 6
        1 3 5 1 3        1 3 1 3        1 3 1 3 5 1 3        1 3 1 3        1 3 1 3 5        1 3 1 3
    2 4 6        2 4 2 4        2 4 2 4        2 4 6        2 4 2 4        2 4 2 4        2 4 6       2 4 6 2 4
```

```
1 3 5        1 1
        2 4 2
    1 3 1 3
2 4 6 2 4       2
```


19.
"Boston". *10 ESFT, Sun Sup 1896.*

```
    2 4 6      2 4 6       2 4 6      2 4 6       2 4 6      2 4 6       2 4        2 4        2 4        2 4 6      2 4 6        2 4 6      2 4 6
1 3 1 3 5 1 3 1 3 5        1 3 5 1 3 1 3 5        1 3 5 1 3 1 3 5                                    1 3 5 1 3 1 3 5        1 3 5 1 3 1 3 5
2 4        2 4        2 4 6      2 4       2 4 6      2 4       2 4 6      2 4 6      2 4 6      2 4 6      2 4       2 4 6      2 4
            1 3 5            1 3 5            1 3 5 1 3 1 3 5 1 3 1 3 5 1 3 1 3 5 1 3 5        1 3 5
```

```
    2 4 6       2 4 6
    1 3 5 1 3 1 3 5
2 4 6       2 4
1 3 5
```

---

18. Left to right, standard, condensed #2. See also Rose #217. Similar to Atwater's Blooming Leaf.

19. Left to right, standard, condensed #2. See also Rose #120. Similar to Atwater's Cloudless Beauty and Missouri Check.

20.
"This Is Sumthing Like Bricks and Blocks". *2 for the big block, 4 for the little one.*

```
                8       8       8                   8           8       8
    2 4 2 4 2 4       2 4 2 4 6 2 4 2 4 6 2 4 2 4 6 2 4        2 4 2 4 2 4        2 4 2 4 6 2 4 2 4 6 2 4 2 4 6 2 4        2 4 2 4
    1 3 1 3      1 3 1 3        1 3 5     1 3 5     1 3 5        1 3 1 3      1 3 1 3        1 3 5     1 3 5     1 3 5        1 3 1 3
2 4 2 4          2 4 2 4                        2 4 2 4        2 4 2 4                            2 4 2 4
1 3        1 3          1 3 1 3      1 3        1 3        1 3 1 3        1 3          1 3 1 3      1 3        1 3        1 3 1 3        1 3
```

```
          8               8       8               8       8       8       8       8       8       8
2 4          2 4 2 4 6 2 4 2 4 6 2 4 2 4 6 2 4        2 4 2 4 2 4        2 4 6     2 4 6     2 4 6     2 4 6     2 4 6     2 4 6
1 3 1 3          1 3 5     1 3 5     1 3 5          1 3 1 3      1 3 1 3
    2 4 2 4                        2 4 2 4          2 4 2 4      2 4       2 4       2 4       2 4       2 4
        1 3 1 3      1 3          1 3          1 3 1 3          1 3      1 3 1 3 5 1 3 1 3 5 1 3 1 3 5 1 3 1 3 5 1 3 1 3 5 1 3 1 3 5
```

21.
"Brush Valley". *Sun Sup. 1896*

```
                                                        2 4 6       2 4     2 4       2 4 6
    1     1     1     1     1     1     1     1            1 3 5     1 3     1 3 5         1 3 5       1 3 5
2 4 6 2 2 4 6 2 2 4 6 2 2 4 6 2 2 4 6 2 2 4 6 2 2 4 6 2 2 4 6 2 2 4 6       2 4 6     2 4     2 4 6       2 4 6 2 4 6 2 4 6 2 4 6 2 4 6
1 3 5     1 3 5     1 3 5     1 3 5     1 3 5     1 3 5     1 3 5     1 3 5     1 3 5 1 3 5         1 3     1 3         1 3 5 1 3 5       1 3 5       1 3 5
```

```
2 4 6        2 4     2 4       2 4 6
    1 3 5       1 3     1 3 5
    2 4 6       2 4     2 4 6
1 3 5        1 3     1 3       1 3 5
```

20. Left to right, standard, condensed #2. Because of the placement of 8s on the fifth line, we can assume that this is a four-shaft draft which could be enlarged by making those marked blocks eight threads long instead of four or six. The pattern is similar to Butternut with a Table, to Nine Stars & Table, and to Perry's Victory.

21. Left to right, standard, condensed #2. Draft begins on the lowest row. The pattern is related to Atwater #48, King's Flower.

22.

"Buckens And Owels". *Sun Sup. 1896, quite dirty. W.W. Fike, Suneyside, WV. Also in duplicate on ad of FSC Wright Apothecary, Wakefield, Aug 13, 1898. (Small M's & O's).*

```
  2 4     2 4     2 4     2 4     2 4     2 4     2 4     2 4     2 4     2 4
1 3       1 3 2 4       1 3 2 4       1 3 2 4       1 3 2 4       1 3
  1 3 2 4       1 3 2 4       1 3 2 4       1 3 2 4       1 3 2 4     2 4
2 4     1 3     1 3     1 3     1 3     1 3     1 3     1 3     1 3     1 3
```

23.

"Catalpa Flower". *On gray cardboard back of Eureka Carpet Warp ad.*

```
    2   1   1                        2   2   1   6 2 2 2 2 2 2
  1 1 2 2 2 2 6   2   2   2   2   2   2   2   1 1 1 1 2 2 6     1   1   1
6 6   1   1   1 1 1 1 1 1 1 1 1 1 1 1 1 1 1 1 2 6   2   1   1 1
1                 2   2   2   2   2   2   2   2   1         6 1   1   1   1
```

24.

"Catalpa Flower from Tenn." *on piece of brown paper, fairly recent.*

```
6 2 2 2 2 2 6     2   2   2                          4 2     4 2     4 2
  2   2   2     6 2 2 2 2 2 6   2   2   2   2   2   2   2   6 3 1 3 1 3 1 3 1 3 1 5 3 1
          6 6   2   2   6 2 2 2 2 2 2 2 2 2 2 2 2 2 2 2 6     4 2     4 2     6 4 2 6 4 2
6   2   2   6 6         2   2   2   2   2   2   2   2                          5 3 1
```

[A corrected version of Catalpa Flower, taken from Atwater, p. 202, is inserted here on the original.]

---

22. Left to right, standard, condensed #2. If the final (right) block of four threads is omitted and the first (left) block of four threads is inverted, the draft is five repeats of a small all over pattern. It can be woven as M's & O's (as marked), but if woven as overshot, it is the same as Atwater's #3, Turkey Foot.

23. Left to right, standard, condensed #2. The final (right) 2 should be a 6, This is the same as Rose #24.

24. Right to left, standard, condensed #3. Same as Atwater #143, Work Complete or Catalpa Flower. A corrected version of Catalpa Flower, taken from Atwater, p. 202, is inserted here on the original.

25.
"Chpmans Fancey", Block Pattern. *Each block has a border. On very dirty brown paper.*

```
  3 1 3 1   3 1    1    1    1    1    1    1    1    1    3 1   3 1 3 1       4 2       3 1       4 2
      4 2           4 2 6 4 2 6 4 2 6 4 2 6 4 2 6 4 2 6 4 2       4 2 3   1 3 1   2   4 2 3   1 3 1
  2            1   3 1   3 1   3 1   3 1   3 1   3 1   3 1   3 1   3 1       1           2       3 1       2
  3   1       4 2 6 4 2                                       4 2 6 4 2
```

```
  3 1   3 1   3 1   3 1   3 1   3 1   3 1   3 1    1           2       3 1       2       4 2       3 1       4 2
                                            4 2 6 4 2                           3 1   2   4 2 3   1 3 1
  1    1    1    1    1    1    1    1   3 1   3 1 3 1       4 2       3 1       4 2   3   1       2
  6 4 2 6 4 2 6 4 2 6 4 2 6 4 2 6 4 2 6 4 2 6 4 2       4 2 3   1 3 1   2   4 2 3   1 3 1
```

```
      3   1       2       3 1       1   3 1
                                  4 2 6 4 2
  4 2       3 1       4 2       3 1 3 1   3 1
  3 1   2   4 2 3   1 3 1   2   4 2               4 2
```

25. Right to left, standard, condensed #3. The pattern is a flawed Patch type.

26.
"Chariot Wheeles". *North Carolina.*

```
42  42  42  42  42    4266  42  64242          4266  42  6426424 2
 6   6   6   6  42       6   6         42642       6   8                 42642
3113113113113 1          1          31        1      1                  531          531
                    3131  113111    3131  3131  113115311 1113131
```

27.
"Chairiot Wheeles". *On mussed brown paper.*

```
    1 3        1 3        1 3        1 3        1 3      1 3 1 3 1 3 5 7 1 3 1 3 5 7 1 3 5 7           1 3              1 3 5 7
1 3 5 7    1 3 5 7    1 3 5 7    1 3 5 7    1 3 5 7    1 3 5 7                                  1 3 5 7    1 3 5 7
2 4 6 8 2 4 2 4 6 8 2 4 2 4 6 8 2 4 2 4 6 8 2 4 2 4 6 8 2 4 2 4 6 8 2 4    2 4 6 8    2 4 6 8
                                                                       2 4        2 4        2 4 6 8 2 4 6 8 2 4 2 4 6 8 2 4 6 8
```

```
1 3 5 7 1 3                1 3 1 3 5 7 1 3 5 7        1 3           1 3 5 7 1 3 5 7
        1 3 1 3 5 7 1 3              1 3 5 7      1 3 5 7
2 4 6 8       2 4 6 8       2 4 6 8                       2 4 6 8
        2 4 2 4       2 4 2 4       2 4 6 8 2 4 6 8 2 4 2 4 6 8 2 4 6 8
```

28.
"Charriot Wheeles".

```
    1 3   1 3   1 3   1 3   1 3   1 3 1 3 1 1 3 1 1   1 3   1 3        1 3 1 1   1 3   1 1
1 3   1     1     1     1     1                       1     1    1 3 1 1 3       1     1
2    2 4 8 2 4 8 2 4 8 2 4 8 2 4 8 2 4 8 2 4    8    8              8       8          8
                              2 4   2 4   8 8 2 4 8 2 4 2 4   2 4 2 6   8 8 2 4 8 8
```

29.
(marked good).

```
   1            2              6 4 2 6 4 2 6 4 2 4 2 6 4 2 5 3 1 5 3 1           3   1          1              2
       2   3   1 4 2      5 3 1 5 3 1      5 3 1     5 3 1     6 4 2 6 4 2        2   3   1          2   3   1
3   1    2   3   1      6 4 2 6 4 2                  5 3 1 5 3 1         2   3   1   2   3   1
2   2 3   1       3 1 5 3 1       5 3 1     3 1     4 2     5 3 1 6 4 2 5 3 1       2   2 3   1
```

```
4 2          3   1 1   2        4 2 3   1        1           2   4 2    3   1 1   2        4 2 3   1
      3   1   2   3   1   2        2   3   1          2   3   1    3   1   2   3   1   2        2   3   1
   3   1   2         3   1   2        2   3   1   2   3   1      3   1   2         3   1   2              2
3 1   2           2        3   1 3 1       2   2 3   1       3 1   2       2                3   1 3 1
```

---

26. Right to left, historical, condensed #3. The wheels are lopsided. See also Rose #28, #33, #36, #102, #168, #169, #243 and #244; also Atwater #84, Double Chariot Wheels or Church Windows.

27. Left to right, historical, condensed #2. This pattern is similar to Rose #26, except the wheels are partial.

28. Left to right, historical, condensed #3. Another variant of Rose #26 with incomplete wheels framing the table.

29. Right to left, standard, condensed #2. In the 14th and 15th column from the left, the 4 and 2 should be in the top row. The pattern is listed as Weaver Rose's Single Chariot Wheel in Atwater #77, and is similar to Atwater #16, Crown and Diamond.

30.
"Checker Board". *1896*

```
                                              1 3 5 1 3 5    1 3    1 3 5 1 3 5
  2 4    2 4    2 4    2 4    2 4    2 4    2 4         2 4 6    2 4    2 4 6
1 3 1 3 1 3 1 3 1 3 1 3 1 3 1 3 1 3 1 3 1 3 1 3 1 3 1 3     1 3    1 3
2 4    2 4    2 4    2 4    2 4    2 4    2 4    2 4 2 4 6      2 4    2 4    2 4 6
```

31.
"China Leaves Large". *On white pasteboard.*

```
7 5 3 1           3 1    3 1    3 1                       6 4 2 4 2
  6 4 2 7 5 3 1                               6 4 2 7 5 3 1
    6 4 2 7 5 3 1    3 1    3 1    6 4 2 7 5 3 1
      6 4 2 4 2 4 2 4 2 4 2 4 2 7 5 3 1                3 1
```

32.
"China Leaves". *On white pasteboard.*

```
D B      B   B   B         D B B
c a c a                   c a c a
  D B D B   B   B   D B D B
    c a a a a a a c a         a
```

```
                                     ┌────────── repeat ──────────┐
4      4              4 4 4 │4 4 4            4      4      4          4 4 4
               3  3  3  3  │3  3  3  3                            3  3  3  3
   2    2  2  2  2          │        2  2  2  2    2      2    2  2  2  2
 1  1  1  1  1             1│         1  1  1  1  1  1  1  1  1  1  1            1
```

---

30. Left to right, standard, condensed #2. See also Rose #31, #32 and #166. Similar to Atwater's Butternut, Cross of Tennessee and King's Delight.

31. Right to left.

32. Right to left, standard, condensed #2. The lettered draft is original. The bottom line is a modern translation of it (the first 36 threads constitute a repeat). There is an error in the translation; the 20th column from the right should be a 3, not a 1. The pattern is a finer version of Rose #31.

33.

"Double Chariot Wheels or Church Windows". #1.

```
   3 1        3 1        3 1       3 1 3 1      5 3 1 3 1 5 3 1      3 1 3 1      3 1 3 1      5 3 1 3 1 5 3 1      3 1 3 1        3 1
6 4 2 4 2 6 4 2 4 2 6 4 2 4 2 6 4 2 4 2              4 2        4 2 4 2 4 2                                                   4 2 6 4 2 4 2
5 3 1     5 3 1     5 3 1     5 3 1       5 3 1             5 3 1       3 1       5 3 1           5 3 1        5 3 1
                         4 2 6 4 2 6 4 2      6 4 2 6 4 2 4 2        4 2 6 4 2 6 4 2 4 2 6 4 2 6 4 2 4 2
```

```
   3 1        3 1        3 1
6 4 2 4 2 6 4 2 4 2 6 4 2 4 2
5 3 1     5 3 1     5 3 1
```

34.

"Church WINDoWs". #2. *Duplicate on very dirty cardboard. Sun. Suppl. 1896.*

```
    1 1      1   3 6   2   1 1   3     2 2      6
   2 2      2   2     1 3     2 1     1 1      1 1 1 1 1 1 1 1 1 1 1 1
  2    1   1 1                  2 2      2 2   4 2 2 2 2 2 2 2 2 2 2 2 2 2 2 2 2 2 2 2 2 2 2 4
 1   3    2 3       1      6        1 1     1 1 1 1 1 1 1 1 1 1 1 1 1 1 1 1
```

```
6      2 2         1   3 6   2   1 1   3     2 2
   1 1   3 1   3   2     1 3     2 1      1 1
  2 2     1   2                    2 2      2
 1 1    1          1      6        1 1
```

35.

"Charriot Wheels and Church Windows". #3. *On brown paper.*

```
        1                 1     1 1      1 1 1 1 1      1 1 1      1                         1
 2     2     2       2   2   2   2   2     4 4   8 8      8   8      8 8   4 4     2   2   2   2   2   2      2   2   2   2
1 1 1 1 1 1 1    1 1 1 1 1 1 1 1 1 1 1 1    1 1        1 1          1 1        1 1   1 1 1 1 1 1 1 1 1 1 1 1 1 1 1 1    1 1 1 1 1 1 1
 2   2   2   2 4 2   2   2   2   2   2   2 4 4      4      8 8   4   8 8      8      4 4 2   2   2   2   2   2   2 4 2   2   2   2
```

---

33. Right to left, standard, condensed #2. In the 16th and 17th columns from the right in the first line, the 2 and 4 should be on the third row up, not the lowest row. The pattern is different from the one Atwater calls Church Windows (#84). See Rose #26.

34. Standard, condensed #3. There is an error in the 52nd column from the left; the 1 and 2 should each be one row lower, on the lowest and second rows instead of the second and third. Neither this pattern not the following one is the same as Atwater's Church Windows; it is almost identical to Rose #151.

35. Standard, condensed #1.

36.
"Chariot Wheels". *South Carolina, on end of cardboard box.*

```
4 2   4 2   4 2   4 2   4 2      4 2 6 6   4 2      6 4 2 4 2         4 2 6 6   4 2   6 4 2 6 4 2 4 2
  6     6     6     6     4 2       6       6        4 2 6 4 2          6       6                  4 2 6 4 2
3 1 1 3 1 1 3 1 1 3 1 1 3 1         1               3 1       1         1                5 3 1       5 3 1
                    3 1 3 1   1 1 3 1 1 3 1      3 1 3 1   3 1 3 1   1 1 3 1 1 5 3 1        3 1 3 1
```

37.
"Cumpass #3". *Sun. Suppl. 1896.*

```
      4 2 4 2     4 2   4 2 1 2   4 2     4 2     1 2 4 2   4 2         4 2           4 2
  3 1 3 1                    1 1   3 1 3 1 3 1 5 3 1   1           3 1 3 1 3 1
4 2 4 2         4 2     4 2       1 6   4 2   6 4 2         4 2     4 2 4 2     4 2 4 2
1 3         3 1 3 1 3 1 3 1 1 3                     3 1 3 1 3 1 3 1             3 1 3 1
```

38.
"Cumpas #2". *Sun Suppl. 1896.*

```
6 4 2 6 4 2 6 4 2 6 4 2              6 4 2 6 4 2     6 4 2       6 4 2     6 4 2 6 4 2 6 4 2
5 3 1       5 3 1           5 3 1           5 3 1 5 3 1         5 3 1     5 3 1     5 3 1         5 3 1       5 3 1
                  6 4 2 6 4 2 6 4 2         6 4 2       6 4 2 6 4 2       6 4 2                 6 4 2 6 4 2 6 4 2 6 4 2 5 3 1
    5 3 1       5 3 1 5 3 1       5 3 1 5 3 1               5 3 1 5 3 1       5 3 1     5 3 1     5 3 1 5 3 1       5 3 1       6 4 2
```

```
6 4 2 6 4 2 6 4 2
    5 3 1

5 3 1       5 3 1
```

39.
"Cumpass Work". *Rhobert Northrop. Sept. 8, 1795. Also Daniel Pierees Compass Work on Sun. Suppl.*

```
2 4         2 4 2 4 2 4       2 4 2 4             2 4 6 2 4 2 4 6 2 4 2 4 6 2 4 2 4 6 2 4 2 4 6           2 4 2 4
        1 3 1 3       1 3 1 3         1 3 1 3     1 3     1 3 1 3 5     1 3 5     1 3 5     1 3 5     1 3 5 1 3     1 3     1 3 1 3
    2 4 2 4         2 4 2 4         2 4 2 4 2 4 2 4                                             2 4 2 4 2 4 2 4         2 4
1 3 1 3         1 3         1 3 1 3         1 3     1 3         1 3     1 3     1 3     1 3         1 3     1 3         1 3 1 3
```

```
    2 4 2 4 2 4         2 4 2 4
1 3 1 3     1 3 1 3         1 3
2 4         2 4 2 4
        1 3         1 3 1 3
```

36. Historical, condensed #3. Error: delete the 3 from the 32nd column from the right, and close the gap. See Rose #26.

37. Right to left (one line). Standard, condensed #3. In the 20th and 33rd columns from the right, instead of a 1 in the top row there should be a 4 above a 3 in the top two rows. In the 30th column from the right, there should be a 1 above a 6 in the middle two rows. In the 34th and 35th and in the 48th and 49th columns from the right, the 1 and 3 should be transposed.

38. Right to left, standard, condensed #2.

39. Left to right, standard, condensed #2.

40.
"Summer and Winter Cumpass Work Draft".

```
                                                          2 4 6 8      2 4 6 8
                                      2 4 6 8 10 12              2 4            2 4 6 8 10 12
              2 4      2 4      2 4            2 4 6 8 10 12                              2 4 6 8        2 4 6 8
2 4 6 8 10 12 14 16 18 20    2 4      2 4      2 4 6 8 10 12                                    2 4
  3    7    11    15    19 3  3  3  3  3  3  7    11   3  7    11   3  7    11   3  7   3   3   7   3   7   11   3   7   3   3   7
  1    5    9    13    17 1   1   1   1   1   1   5   9    1   5   9    1   5   9    1   5   1   1   5   1   5   9    1   5   1   1   5
```

```
2 4 6 8      2 4 6 8
    2 4            2 4 6 8 10 12
                   2 4 6 8 10 12              2 4      2 4      2 4                              2 4
                                 2 4 6 8 10 12          2 4      2 4      2 4 6 8 10 12 14 16 18 20    2 4
  3    7    3   3   7   3   7    11   3   7    11   3   7    11   3   3   3   3   3   7    11    15    19 3
  1    5    1   1   5   1   5   9    1   5   9    1   5   9    1   1   1   1   1   1   5   9    13    17    1
```

41.
"Coverlet #4".

```
  4      4      4 4 4          4      4      4 4 4          4      4      4        2-4
    3 3 3 3          3          3 3 3 3          3          3 3 3 3                2-3
      2      2 2 2    2          2      2 2 2 2    2      2      2                  3-4
  1              1 1 1 1                    1 1 1 1                                2-3
                                                                                  3-4
                                                                                  1-4
                                                                                  1-2
                                                                                  1-3
                                                                                  1-2
                                                                                  1-4
                                                                                  2-4
                                                                                  3-4
                                                                                  2-3
```

42.
"The Cross". *On dirty brown paper. Duplicate on grey cardboard back of adv. Eureka Carpet Warp.*

```
|Begin
                                        1 3 5 1 3 5      1 3 1 3      1 3 1 3 1 3      1 3 1 3
  2 4      2 4      2 4      2 4      2 4      2 4      2 4      2 4 2 4 6      2 4 2 4      2 4 2 4      2 4 2 4
1 3 1 3 1 3 1 3 1 3 1 3 1 3 1 3 1 3 1 3 1 3 1 3 1 3 1 3 1 3 1 3      1 3 1 3      1 3 1 3      1 3 1 3      1 3 1 3
  2 4      2 4      2 4      2 4      2 4      2 4      2 4      2 4 6 2 4      2 4 2 4      2 4      2 4 2 4      2 4
```

```
1 3 5 1 3 5
      2 4 6

2 4 6
```

40. Left to right, 60 blocks. Standard, condensed #2. A summer & winter weave, same pattern at Rose #146 in a different scale. See Atwater #196, Mosaics.

41. Left to right, mixed style, modern. The draft doesn't make sense as it is. It is a mixture of "historical" and "standard" notations. If the 2s and the 11th and 13th columns from the left are dropped to 1s and the 3 in the 18th column is raised to 4, the first 20 threads become a small repeat similar to Rose #6 and Atwater #4.

42. Left to right, standard, condensed #2. Similar to Atwater #11, Cross of Tennessee.

43.

"Cross and Diamonds Coverlet". *5 Harnesses, 5 Treadles. Treadles 1 & 5 are plain weave. Left foot is always on treadle 5. Treadles 2-3-4 form the pattern. Half the threads are on Harness 5.*
Tie 4-5 to treadle 1.
Tie 3-5 to treadle 2.
Tie 2-5 to treadle 3.
Tie 1-5 to treadle 4.
Tie 1-2-3-4 to treadle 5.

```
                                                                              Tread.
                                                                              a b c d e
                          1   1                      1   1              1   1   2 3 1 2 1
              1   1            1   1                      1   1      1   1       5 5 5 5 5
          1   1                        1   1                  1   1             2 3 1 2 1
  1   1   1   1                            1   1   1   1                        5 5 5 5 5
  1 1 1 1 1 1 1 1 1 1 1 1 1 1 1 1 1 1 1 1 1 1 1 1 1 1 1 1 1 1 1 1 1 1 1        5 2 4 3 1
                                                                               5 5 5 5 5
                          Barley Corn. 5 Harness                               3 2 4 3 1
                                                                               5 5 5 5 5
                                                                               4 1 3 4
                                                                               5 5 5
                                                                               4 1 3 4
                                                                               5 5 5
```

44.

"Crosswise Ireland". *Adv. 1769. On very stained brown paper. Monk's Belt.*

```
8   8   8   2   2   8   8   8     6   6     6   6   6   6   6   6   6     6   6
  2   2   8   8   8   2   2   24    2   24    2   2   2   2   2   2   24    2   8
1   1   1   1   1   1   1   1       1   1       1   1   1   1   1   1   1       1   1
  1   1   1   1   1   1   1   13    1   13    1   1   1   1   1   1   13    1   1
```

45.

"Crown of Diamonds". *On box card board.*

```
4   4   4   4   4   4                   4   4   4   4   4   4   4   4   4   4                4   4   4
          3   3   3   3   3   3                           3   3   3   3   3   3
2   2   2                   2   2   2   2   2   2                   2   2   2   2   2   2
          1   1   1   1   1   1           1   1   1   1   1   1           1   1   1   1   1   1
```

```
X   X X             4   4   4           4   4   4
X X       X           3   3   3   3   3   3     3   3   3   3   3   3
X   X   X           2   2   2                   2   2   2
X   X   X           1   1   1     1   1   1   1   1   1   1   1   1
```

---

43. Either direction, ones, modern.   A spot Bronson or barley corn weave. When making the tie-up, 5 is the lowest shaft and 1 the highest in the draft. The note concerning the treadles is true only if treadle 1 is not used. To weave the pattern as drawn in, a sixth treadle (tied to shaft 5 only) is needed. The block pattern is a diaper (diamonds), and the treadling given weaves stripes of alternating diamonds and crosses separated by stripes of plain weave.

44. Left to right, historical, condensed #3. See also Rose #19, #120 and #162. The pattern is similar to Atwater #127 and #130, Cloudless Beauty and Missouri Check.

45. Left to right, historical, modern. There is an error in the tie-up given; the single ✕s in the second and top rows should be lined up vertically in the same column. That makes the left two columns the tabby treadles and the other four columns the pattern treadles. This pattern is not the same as Atwater's Crown and Diamonds, #16. It is a flawed double diamond.

46.
"Crown and Dimons". *Rhobert Northrup, 1815. On piece of box card board.*

```
      4   4   4   4   4              4   4   4          4   4          4   4   4                              4   4   4
        3   3   3   3   3                                                                3   3   3   3   3   3
  2   2                2   2   2   2          2   2   2          2   2   2          2   2   2   2   2   2
    1   1   1   1          1   1   1   1   1   1   1   1   1   1   1   1   1   1   1   1   1   1   1   1
```

```
  4   4              4   4   4   4   4
        3   3   3   3        3   3   3
      2   2   2   2              2   2
    1   1   1   1        1              1
```

47.
"Demons Fancy". *April 11, 1815. On brown paper.*

```
          4   4          4   4          4   4          4   4          4   4
        3   3   3   3   3        3   3   3   3   3        3   3   3   3   3        3   3   3   3   3        3   3   3   3
  2   2   2   2        2   2   2   2   2        2   2   2   2   2        2   2   2   2        2   2   2   2
    1   1          1   1          1   1          1   1          1   1
```

```
          4   4          4   4          4   4      4      4   4                      4   4      4          4   4
        3   3   3   3   3        3   3   3   3   3          3          3          3   3          3          3
  2   2   2   2        2   2   2   2   2        2   2   2          2          2          2   2   2   2          2          2
    1   1          1   1          1   1   1   1          1          1   1   1          1   1   1   1   1      1          1   1   1
```

```
          4   4                      4   4
  3   3          3   3   3   3   3          3   3   3   3   3
    2   2   2   2   2        2   2   2   2   2          2
      1   1          1   1
```

48.
"Dewey's Fancey".

```
1 3 5      1      1 3 5 2 4   2 4 1 3 5      1      1 3 5 2 4   2 4 1 3 5      1      1 3 5 1 3    1 3      1 3      1 3      1 3
                  1 3 1 3 1 3          1      1 3 1 3 1 3                      2 4 2 4 2 4 2 4 2 4 2 4 2 4 2 4
    1 3 5   1 3 5          2 4      1 3 5   1 3 5          2 4      1 3 5   1 3 5          1 3      1 3      1 3      1 3
2 4 6 2 4 6 2 2 4 6 2 4 6            2 4 6 2 4 6 2 2 4 6 2 4 6            2 4 6 2 4 6 2 2 4 6 2 4 6
```

```
    1 3      1 3
2 4 2 4 2 4 2 4
1 3      1 3
```

---

46. Right to left, standard, modern. See also Rose #17, #165 and #210, and Atwater #10A, Single Orange Peel.

47. Right to left, standard, modern. Error: delete the 1 that is directly below the 4 in the 12th column from the right, 2nd line. See also Rose #55, #160, #213 and #239 for different versions of this pattern, which is a table of diamonds with cross division.

49.
"The Dimond and Crown".

```
2                1           1  3 2 4              1 3 5 7 1 3 5 7 2 4 6 8 2 4 2 4 6 8 2 4 6 8 2 4 6 8                    2 4
1  3  2              1  3  2          2 4 6 8 2 4 6 8        1 3 5 7        1 3 5 7          1 3 5 7 1 3 5 7                    2
   1  3  2    1  3  2      1 3 5 7 1 3 5 7                                            2 4 6 8 2 4 6 8   2 4 3  1
   1   32 2       1 3 2 4 6 8            2 4 6 8        1 3        1 3 5 7              1 3 5 7 1 3 1 3
```

```
2   2 1               2   2 3  1        1   3   2              1   3 2 4      1 3 2 4 2 4
1  2 3  1        2  3  1    2  3 1        1   3   2        1   3   2      1 3 2 4      1 3 1 3
     2  4 2  2  3  1        2  3  1        1  3  2    1  3  2        1 3 2 4        2 4 2 4
1          3 1 3  1            1          2        2        1   3 2  2        1 3 2 4        1 3          1 3
```

50.
"DiaMoNDS".

```
        4 2
     4 2    4 2
  4 2              4 2
                      4 2
  3 3 3 3 3 3
  1 1 1 1 1 1
```

51.
A duplicate draft continues with this.

```
8 6 4 2         4 2       8 6 4 2                                      4 2
        8 6 4 2     8 6 4 2                              4 2    4 2
                                          4 2    4 2            4 2    4 2
                                       4 2    4 2                4 2    4 2
7   3   7   3     37   3   7   3           3 3 3 3 3 3 3 3 3 3 3
5   1   5   1   1   5   1   5   1          1 1 1 1 1 1 1 1 1 1 1
```

52.
No name on this. Looks like a diamond, done on back of Sun. Suppl. 1896.

```
        4 2                    4 2    8 6 4 2 4 2
     4 2    4 2              4 2    4 2            4 2
  4 2              4 2    4 2                    4 2    4 2
4 2                            4 2            4 2    4 2
  3 3 3 3 3 3 3 3 3 3 37 3     3 3 3 3 3 373
  1 1 1 1 1 1 1 1 1 1 1 5 1 1 1 1 1 1 1 151
```

48. Left to right, standard, condensed #2. Same as Rose #223 and Atwater #57. When woven as drawn in or "star fashion", it is Nine Stars and Table; when treadled "rose fashion", it is Nine Snowballs or Nine Roses.

49. Left to right, standard, condensed #3. Pattern is a very flawed version of a wheel and diamond design similar to Atwater #79 and #80B, Lover's Knot and Chariot Wheel.

50. Right to left, standard, condensed #2. A simple diamond pattern in summer & winter weave with four-thread blocks.

51. Right to left, standard, condensed #2. Another four-thread block summer & winter weave. It is similar to, but simpler than, Atwater #180C, Fish in the Pond.

52 & 53. Right to left, standard, condensed #2. Summer & winter four-thread blocks. In both drafts, the 2 and 4 threads are missing; presumably those threads should be on the 4th row up from the bottom. Both patterns are diamonds with flaws.

53.
Border to Weaver Johns draft. *Looks like above corrected, on dirty brown paper.*

```
       4 2               4 2               4 2          4 2
     4 2     4 2            4 2     4 2       4 2   8 6 4 2      4 2
   4 2           4 2   4 2        4 2   4 2               4 2   4 2
 4 2          4 2             4 2                    4 2    4 2
 3 3 3 3 3 3 3 3 3 3 3 3 3 3 3 3 3 7 3   3 3 3 3 3 3 3 3 7 3
 1 1 1 1 1 1 1 1 1 1 1 1 1 1 1 1 1 5 1 1 1 1 1 1 1 1 1 5 1
```

54.
Diamond Huckerback.

```
         5 3 1     5 3 1              5 3 1     5 3 1
           4 2       4 2               4 2       4 2
               4 2                       4 2
             5 3 1                     5 3 1
 5 3 1     5 3 1          5 3 1     5 3 1
 4 2       4 2            4 2       4 2
     4 2                    4 2
   5 3 1                  5 3 1
```

55.
"Diman's Fancy". *1821, old and dirty piece of foolscap used.*

```
    2   8 4 4 2        3 1          3 1          3 1          3 1          3 1
          7 3       2  4 2 3  1   2  4 2 3  1      4 2 3  1   2  4 2 3  1   2  4 2
 3   1    6 2    4 2 3 1   2  4 2 3 1  2  4 2 3 1  2  4 2 3 1  2  4 2 3 1
   2   3   1 5 1 3 1 3 1        3 1         3 1  2      3 1           3 1
```

```
              3 1          3  1         3 1          3 1          3 1 5 1 3 1
 3   1     2  4 2 3  1   2    2  3  1  2  4 2 3  1   2  4 2 3  1      6 2           3 1
 2  4 2 3  1   2  4 2 3  1      2  4 2 3  1   2  4 2 3  1   2  3  1    7 3      2  4 2
   3 1          3 1           3 1          3 1              2  4 2 8 4 4 2 3  1
```

56.
"The Dog Track". *On a little piece of brown paper.*

```
 4 2     4 2     4 2 4 2     4 2      4 2
                   3 1 3 1 3 1 3 1 3 1
   4 2     4 2            4 2     4 2
 3 1 3 1 3 1 3 1
```

---

54. Right to left, standard, condensed #2. Huck weave. The first 30 threads constitute a repeat.

55. Right to left, standard, condensed #2. The pattern is a flawed version of Rose #47, Demon's Fancy.

56. Right to left, standard, condensed #2. The same as Atwater #37, Dog Tracks, when treadled rose fashion.

57.

```
4  4  4 4  4  4
          1 1 1 1 1
4  4     4  4
1 1 1 1 1
```

58.
"Dog TRAD". *On dirty cardboard.*

```
2 4     2 4     2 4 2 4     2 4     2 4
                1 3 1 3 1 3 1 3 1 3
   2 4     2 4         2 4     2 4
1 3 1 3 1 3 1 3 1 3
```

59.
"Double Bow Knot". *Also done in 6 instead of 8.*

```
2 4         2 4 6 2 4 6              2 4 6 8 2 4 6 8      2 4 6 8 2 4 6 8      2 4 6 2 4 6          2 4 6
1 3 1 3         1 3 5 1 3 5           1 3 5 7 1 3 5 7      1 3 5 7 1 3 5 7      1 3 5 1 3 5          2 4 6
   2 4 2 4         2 4 6 2 4 6           2 4 6 8 2 4 6 8      2 4 6 8 2 4 6 8      2 4 6 2 4 6
      1 3 1 3 5         1 3 5 7 1 3 5 7      1 3 5 7 1 3 5 7      1 3 5 7 1 3 5      1 3 5 1 3 5
```

```
2 4         2 4 6 8        2 4 2 4 6      2 4 6 8 2 4 6 8      2 4 6 8 2 4 6 8      2 4 6 8 2 4 6 8
1 3 1 3         1 3 1 3        1 3 5 1 3 5 7      1 3 5 7 1 3 5 7      1 3 5 7 1 3 5 7
   2 4 2 4         2 4 2 4         2 4 6 2 4 6          2 4 6 8 2 4 6 8      2 4 6 8 2 4 6 8      2 4 6 8
      1 3 1 3 5 7 1 3         1 3 5 1 3 5      1 3 5 7 1 3 5 7      1 3 5 7 1 3 5 7      1 3 5 7 1 3 5 7
```

```
      2 4 6 8 2 4 6 8            2 4 6 8 2 4 6 8        2 4 6 2 4 6      2 4 2 4 6      2 4 6      2 4 6      2 4 6
1 3 5 7 1 3 5 7            1 3 5 7 1 3 5 7        1 3 5 1 3 5      1 3 1 3
2 4 6 8            2 4 6 8 2 4 6 8          2 4 6 8 2 4 6      2 4 2 4      2 4 6      2 4 6      2 4 6
         1 3 5 7 1 3 5 7            1 3 5 7 1 3 5 7        1 3 5 1 3      1 3 5 1 3 5 1 3 5 1 3 5 1 3 5 1 3 5 1 3 5
```

```
      2 4 6       2 4 6       2 4 6       2 4 6       2 4 6
2 4 6       2 4 6       2 4 6       2 4 6       2 4 6
1 3 5 1 3 5 1 3 5 1 3 5 1 3 5 1 3 5 1 3 5 1 3 5 1 3 5 1 3 5
```

57. The same as #33A, except standard, condensed #1, reading in either direction.

58. Same as #33A, except reading from left to right.

59. Left to right, standard, condensed #2. In the 21st through 24th columns from the left in the first line, the 2, 4, 6, 8 group should be one column to the left, directly over the 1, 3, 5, 7 group, and the resulting 24th column should be deleted. The pattern is similar to Atwater #115, Double Bow Knot.

60.
"Double Bow Knot". *Sun. Suppl. 1896. #2.*

```
2 4 6            2 4 6 2 4 6      2 4 2 4   2 2 4 6 2   2 4 2 4    2 4 6 2 4 6              2 4 6            2 4 6
1 3 5 1 3 5      1 3 5 1 3 5        1 3 1 3     1 1       1 1     1 3 1 3     1 3 5 1 3 5    1 3 5 1 3 5 1 3 5
    2 4 6 2 4 6 2 4 6          2 4 2 4      2 2        2 2     2 4 2 4         2 4 6 2 4 6 2 4 6     2 4 6 2 4 6
        1 3 5          1 3 5 1 3     1 3 1   1 3 5   1 1 3     1 3 1 3 5          1 3 5             1 3 5 1 3 5
```

```
2 4 6           2 4 2    2 4 2 4 6 2 4 2 4 6 2 4 2 4 6 2 4 2 4 6 2 4 2 4 6 2 4 2 4 6 2 4 2 4 6 2 4 2 4   2 2 4       2 4 2 4 6
1 3 5 1 3 5       1 1     1 3 5    1 3 5    1 3 5    1 3 5    1 3 5    1 3 5     1 1      1 3 1 3              1 3 5
    2 4 6 2 4 6     2 2                                                    2 2     2 4 2 4       2 4 6 2 4 6
        1 3 5 1 3    1 1 3    1 3    1 3    1 3    1 3    1 3    1 3 1    1 3 1 3     1 3 5 1 3 5
```

61.
"THE · DOUBLE · BoW NoT", #3.

```
2 4         2 4 6 2 4 6      8 8    8 8    8 8          1 3 5 1 3        1       1 3 1 3 5
1 3 1 3          1 3 5 1 3 5    1 1    1 1    1 2 4 6       2 4 2 4      2 4 2 4            2 4 6
    2 4 2 4           2 4 6 8    8 8    8 8   1 3 5 1 3 5      1 3 1 3   1 3 1 3      1 3 5 1 3 5
        1 3 1 3 5           1 1    1 1    1 1      2 4 6 2 4 6       2 4 8 2 4      2 4 6 2 4 6
```

```
1 1     1 1     1 1        2 4 6 2 4 6      2 4 2 4 6    2 4 6    2 4 6    2 4 6    2 4 6    2 4 6    2 4 6    2 4 6    2 4 6
8    8 8    8 8   1 3 5 1 3 5          1 3 1 3
    1 1     1 1   8 2 4 6          2 4 2 4        2 4     2 4     2 4     2 4     2 4     2 4     2 4     2 4
8 8    8 8    8 1          1 3 5 1 3    1 3 5 1 3 1 3 5 1 3 1 3 5 1 3 1 3 5 1 3 1 3 5 1 3 1 3 5 1 3 1 3 5 1 3 1 3 5 1 3 5
```

62.
"Double Bow Knot or Bow Knot of Mexico". *Tabby (1-3)(2-4). Tread as written.*

```
11  9  7 5 3 1 1     1 1      3 1 1       1 1      1 1          5 3 1 1        3 1 1  1  1  1  1  1  1       5 3 1
                 4 4      6 4 2     10 12      10 10       6 4 2 6 4 2      4 2 4 2
                     1 1      6 1      12 1      1 1      5 3 1 5 3 1       3 1 3 1    1  1  1  1  1  1  5 3 1
        10 8 6 4 2 2 4    6 1       8 1       10 10       8 6 4 2          6 4 2       6 6 6 6 6 6 6 6 6 6 6 6 4 2 6 4 2
```

Center — Reverse to beginning.
Tramp according to figure below and it gives a beautiful figure of diamonds something like this:

---

60. Left to right, standard, condensed #2. This pattern is not a Double Bow Knot, but rather a Blooming Leaf variant similar to Atwater #113.

61. Left to right, standard, condensed #3. This pattern is almost the same as Rose #59.

62. Right to left and reverse. Standard, condensed #3. Similar to Atwater #115, Double Bow Knot.

63.

Probably from Mrs. Allen. Fairly Recent. Atwater p. 191.

Center — Reverse to beginning

4	3 3	4 5	5 6	4 2	3 2		6	3	3	3	3	3	3	3
4 2	3 3	5 5	6 5	2 3		2 2								
2 2	3 4	5 6	5 6	3 3		2 2	3	3	3	3	3	3	3	
	2 3	4 4	6 5	6 4	5 3		2 6 3 3 3 3 3 3 3 3 3 3 3 3 3							

64.

"Emmy Ann Stanton. Diaper." On clean cardboard. Tread as written. Barley Corn Weave.

2 4		2 4		2 4		2 4		2 4	
	2 4		2 4	2 4		2 4		2 4	2 4
		2 4		2 4		2 4		2 4	2 4
1 3 1 3 1 3 1 3 1 3 1 3 1 3 1 3 1 3 1 3 1 3 1 3 1 3 1 3 1 3									

65.

"Every Bodyes Buty".

1	1 1 1	1	1 1 1	1 1		1		1												
	4 4		4 4	8 8		8 8		6	2	2	2	2	2	2	2	2	2	2	2	6
1		1 1		1	1 1	1 1		1 1 1 1 1 1 1 1 1 1 1 1 1 1 1 1 1 1 1 1 1 1 1 1 1 1 1												
4 4	8	4 8 4	8	4 8		8 4 8		8 6	2	2	2	2	2	2	2	2	2	2	2	6

1 1	1	1 1	1 1 1		1	1 1 1	1	
8 8		8 8	4 4			4 4		
	1 1	1 1	1		1	1	1	
8	8 4 8	8 4	8	4 8 4	8	4 4		

66.

"Fading Leaf". On ad for coffee.

1 1	1 3 1 3 5		1 3 5 1 3 5		1 3 5 1 3 5	1 1	1 3 5 1 3 5		1 3 5 1 3 5	1 3 5 1
2 1 1		1 3 5 1 3 5		1 3 5 1 3 5		1 3 1 1 1 3	1 3 5 1 3 5		1 3 5 1 3 5	
1 2 2 2 4		2 4 6 2 4 6		2 4 6 2 4 6		2 2	2 4 6 2 4 6		2 4 6 2 4 6	2
2 2	2 4 6 2 4 6		2 4 6 2 4 6		2 4 6 2 4 2 2 2 2 4 2 4 6		2 4 6 2 4 6		2 4 6 2 4 6	

---

36. Right to left and reverse, standard. A stacked version of #62.

64. Left to right, standard, condensed #1. Spot Bronson weave, concentric diamond or "diaper" pattern.

65. Left to right, standard, condensed #1.

66. Left to right, historical, condensed #2. The pattern is a fractured radiating type.

67.

"THE FEDERAL CITY". *On Sun. Sup. 1896. Duplicate on back of ad for Diamond Blade Sythes.*

```
2 4 6 2 4 2 4 6 2 4 2 4 6 2 4 2 4 6 2 4 2 4 6 2 4 2 4 6 2 4 2 4 6 2 4 2 4 6 2 4 2 4 6 2 4 6         2 4 6           2 4 6
1 3 5     1 3 5     1 3 5     1 3 5     1 3 5     1 3 5     1 3 5     1 3 5     1 3 5     1 3 5     1 3 5     1 3 5     1 3 5
                                                                                        2 4 6 2 4 6     2 4 6 2 4 6
    1 3       1 3       1 3       1 3       1 3       1 3       1 3       1 3       1 3     1 3 5     1 3 5     1 3 5     1 3 5
```

68.

"Fig Leaf or Barren Tree". *From Tenessee on soiled brown paper.*

```
    1 1 3         1 3 1 3 5           2 4 6 8 2 4 6 8         2 4 6 2 4 6     2 4 2 4     2 2 4     2 4     2 4     2 4
    2         2 4 2 4           1 3 5 7 1 3 5 7         1 3 5 7 1 3 5       1 3 1 3     1 1
1 3       1 3 1 3         1 3 5 7 2 4 6 8         2 4 6 8 2 4 6 8         2 4 2 4       2 2       2 4     2 4     2 4
2 4   4 2 4 2       2 4 6 2 4 6 8         1 3 5 7 1 3 5 7         1 3 5 1 3       1 3 1     1 3 1 3 1 3 1 3 1 3 1 3 1 3

    2 4       2 4       2 4     2 4 2     1 3 1 3     1 3 5 1 3 5 7           1 3 5 7 1 3 5 7         1 3 5 1 3         1 3
              1 2         2 4 2 4         2 4 6 8 2 4 6 8           2 4 6 8 2 4 6 8           2 4 2 4
2 4     2 4     2 4     2 4     1 1       1 3 1 3         1 3 5 7 1 3 5 7           1 3 5 7 1 3 5 7         1 3 1 3
1 3 1 3 1 3 1 3 1 3 1 3 1 3     2 2 4       2 4 2 4 6         2 4 6 8 2 4 6 8         2 4 6 8 2 4 6         2 4 2 4

1       1 3 5 7       1 3       1 3 5 7 1 3     1 3 1 3 5 7       1 3         1 3 5 7 1 3     1 3 1 3 5 7         1 3         1 3 5 7
2 2                         2 4 2 4 2 4               2 4 2 4 2 4
    1 1       1 3 5 7     1 3 5 7         1 3           1 3 5 7       1 3 5 7       1 3         1 3 5 7       1 3 5 7
    2 2 4 6 8 2 4 6 8 2 4 2 4 6 8 2 4 6 8         2 4 6 8 2 4 6 8 2 4 2 4 6 8 2 4 6 8         2 4 6 8 2 4 6 8 2 4 2 4 6 8 2 4 6 8
```

```
1 3     1 3 1 3 5 7
2 4 2 4 2 4
    1 3           1 3 5 7
        2 4 6 8 2 4 6 8
```

69.

"THE Flag of our Union". *On Sun. Sup. 1896.*

```
2 4 2 4                             1 3 1 3 1 3 1 3     1 1 1 1 1 1 1 1 1 1     1 3 1 3 1 3 1 3
    1 3 1 3 5       2 4       2 4 6 2 4     2 4     2 4 2 2 2 2 2 2 2 2 2 2 2 2 2 2 2 2 2 2 2 4     2 4     2 4 2 4 6
    2 4 6 1 3 5 1 3 1 3 5 1 3 5             1 1 1 1 1 1 1 1 1 1 1 1 1                1 3 5 1 3 5
1 3       2 4 6     2 4 6         2 4     2 4                             2 4     2 4       2 4 6
```

```
                2 4
2 4       2 4 6 1 3
1 3 1 3 5 1 3 5
    2 4 6
```

---

67. Left to right, standard, condensed #2. Almost the same as Rose #30.

68. Left to right, standard, condensed #2. In the 4th and 5th columns and the 6th and 7th columns from the left, the 2 and 4 are transposed. Except for the error (half a star omitted at the end), this is identical to Atwater #117, Fig Leaf or Wandering Star.

69. Left to right, standard, condensed #2.

70.
"Flowers of Canaan". *A. Stoddard, Groton. March 18, 1827.*

```
                        4 2    4 2    4 2          4 2
                           4 2    4 2        4 2   4 2
                                     4 2          4 2
20 18 16 14 12 10 8 6 4 2              4 2              4 2
19    15    11    7   3   3   3   3   3   3   3   3   3   3   3   3   3
   17    13    9   5   1   1   1   1   1   1   1   1   1   1   1   1   1
```

```
                    20 18 16 14 12 10 8 6 4 2    4 2    20 18 16 14 12 10 8 6 4 2
20 18 16 14 12 10 8 6 4 2                      4 2    4 2
19    15    11    7   3   19    15    11    7   3   3   3   3 19    15    11    7   3
   17    13    9   5   1   17    13    9   5   1   1   1   1   17    13    9   5   1
```

```
4 2    4 2    4 2          4 2          4 2    4 2              4 2          4 2    4 2    4 2
   4 2    4 2          4 2    4 2          4 2          4 2    4 2          4 2    4 2
            4 2          4 2          4 2          4 2          4 2
               4 2          4 2          4 2          4 2
3   3   3   3   3   3   3   3   3   3   3   3   3   3   3   3   3   3   3   3   3   3   3   3   3   3   3   3
1   1   1   1   1   1   1   1   1   1   1   1   1   1   1   1   1   1   1   1   1   1   1   1   1   1   1   1
```

```
20 18 16 14 12 10 8 6 4 2                          4 2    4 2                20 18 16 14 12 10 8 6 4 2
               20 18 16 14 12 10 8 6 4 2    4 2    20 18 16 14 12 10 8 6 4 2
19    15    11    7   3   19    15    11    7   3   3   3   3 19    15    11    7   3   19    15    11    7   3
   17    13    9   5   1   17    13    9   5   1   1   1   1   17    13    9   5   1   17    13    9   5   1
```

```
      4 2              4 2    4 2    4 2
   4 2    4 2              4 2    4 2
4 2              4 2
               4 2
3   3   3   3   3   3   3   3   3   3   3
1   1   1   1   1   1   1   1   1   1   1
```

70. Right to left, standard, condensed #2. Summer & winter weave with four-thread blocks. Almost the same as Atwater #201, Star and Rose. To be symmetrical, the pattern should have additional A, B, C and D blocks at the end.

71.
"4 Leaf Clover". *On ad of Educator Shoes.*

```
        3 1 1      3 1 1   1 1      3 1      3 1 1   1 1      3 1      3 1 1   1 1      3   1 1           2   1              1
      2 4 2      2 4 2      2 4 2          2 4 2      2 4 2          2 4 2      2 4 2          2 3   1          2 4 2
  3   1 1        3 1 1      1   3 1 1      3 1 1      1   3 1 1      3 1 1      1   3 1   2          2   3   1          3 1   2
    2        2 4 2      6 2 8      2 4 2 4 2      8 2 8      2 4 2 4 2      6 2 8        3   1   2          2   3   1        3   1 2
```

```
  3 1      3 1      3 1      3 1      3 1   2          3 1   2
  4 2 4 2 4 2 4 2 4 2 4 2 4 2 4 2 4 2 4 2          2 4 2
    3 1      3 1      3 1      3 1          3   1 1
                              3   1   2          3   1
```

72.
"Fox Trail".

```
  2 6 2 6 2 6 2 6 2 6 2 6 2 6      2      6 2 6      2      6 2 6      2      6 2 6
                        6 6    6 6        6 6    6 6        6 6    6 6
  6    6    6    6    6    6    6 6        6 6    6 6        6 6    6 6          6 6    6
  2    2    2    2    2    2    2      6 2 6      2      6 2 6      2      6 2 6      2
```

73.
"Free Masons Walk". *Sun. Sup. 1896.*

```
  2 4 6 2 4 6        2 4 6 2 4 6                2 4 6 2 4 6        2 4 6 2 4 6                2 4 6 2 4 6        2 4 6        2 4 6
        1 3 5 1 3 5 1 3 5            1 3 5          1 3 5 1 3 5 1 3 5            1 3 5          1 3 5 1 3 5 1 3 5 1 3 5 1 3 5 1 3 5 1 3 5
              2 4 6          2 4 6 2 4 6 2 4 6          2 4 6          2 4 6 2 4 6 2 4 6          2 4 6        2 4 6        2 4 6
  1 3 5              1 3 5 1 3 5        1 3 5 1 3 5                1 3 5 1 3 5        1 3 5 1 3 5
```

```
  2 4 6        2 4 6        2 4 6        2 4 6        2 4 6        2 4 6        2 4 6
  1 3 5 1 3 5 1 3 5 1 3 5 1 3 5 1 3 5 1 3 5 1 3 5 1 3 5 1 3 5 1 3 5 1 3 5 1 3 5 1 3 5
        2 4 6        2 4 6        2 4 6        2 4 6        2 4 6        2 4 6
```

71. Right to left, standard, condensed #3. This is not the same as Atwater's #63, Four Leaf Clover. It is like an Orange Peel pattern with a table added.

72. Right to left, historical, stacked. A star and table pattern.

73. Left to right, standard, condensed #2. A flawed version of Rose #74.

74.
"Free Mason's Walk".

```
6      6 6  6 6      6 6  6  6  6  6  6  6  6  6
  1    1 1 1    1      1 1 1 1 1 1 1 1 1 1 1 1 1 1
  6 6 6    6    6 6 6   6  6  6  6  6  6  6  6
1 1  1 1      1 1   1 1
```
#1.

75.

```
2 4 6 2 4 6      2 4 6 2 4 6              2 4 6 2 4 6      2 4 6 2 4 6        2 4 6 2 4 6    2 4 6      2 4 6
  1 3 5 1 3 5 1 3 5          1 3 5          1 3 5 1 3 5 1 3 5      1 3 5      1 3 5 1 3 5 1 3 5 1 3 5 1 3 5 1 3 5
    2 4 6        2 4 6 2 4 6 2 4 6          2 4 6      2 4 6 2 4 6 2 4 6        2 4 6    2 4 6    2 4 6
1 3 5          1 3 5 1 3 5          1 3 5 1 3 5      1 3 5 1 3 5
```

```
2 4 6      2 4 6      2 4 6      2 4 6      2 4 6      2 4 6      2 4 6
1 3 5 1 3 5 1 3 5 1 3 5 1 3 5 1 3 5 1 3 5 1 3 5 1 3 5 1 3 5 1 3 5 1 3 5 1 3 5
    2 4 6      2 4 6      2 4 6      2 4 6      2 4 6      2 4 6
```
#2.

76.
"Fringe". 20-1, 56' long, finished 4½" deep. About 15 threads, enough to turn over a hem neatly. This centerpiece is overcast on each side. Fringe of old Rose Warp cotton, 5-ply. Any little border pattern. Weave tabby enough for a hem of ⅜", leave a space of 1½".

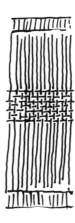

---

74. Reads either way, standard, condensed #1. This pattern is similar to Rose #241 and Atwater #17, John Walker.

75. Left to right, standard, condensed #2. A flawed version of #74.

"Greene Vails". *On cardboard.*

```
3   1      8   8      4 2      8   8      4 2      4 2      4 2      4 2
  2   3   1          3 1 3 1 3 1          3 1 3 1 3 1 3 1 3 1 3 1 3 1 3 1 3 1
    2   8   4 2   8 4 2    4 2 8   4 2   8 4 2    4 2     4 2     4 2     4 2
      1 1 3 1 1 1          1 1 3 1 1 1
```

```
8   4 2   8 4 2    4 2 8   4 2   8 3   1              2   3   1          2   3   1          2   3   1          2   3   1                    2
        3 1 3 1 3 1          2   3   1          2   3   1          2   3   1          2   3   1          2   3   1
8   8      4 2      8   8      2   3   1          2   3   1          2   3   1          2   3   1
1 1 3 1 1 1          1 1 3 1 1 1          2   3   1          2   3   1          2   3   1          2   3 1
```

```
4 2      4 2 8   4 2   8 4 2    4 2     4 2     4 2     4 2     4 2     4 2     4 2     4 2     4 2
3 1 3 1 3 1          3 1 3 1 3 1 3 1 3 1 3 1 3 1 3 1 3 1 3 1 3 1 3 1 3 1 3 1 3 1 3 1 3 1 3 1 3 1 3 1
    4 2      8   8      4 2     4 2     4 2     4 2     4 2     4 2     4 2     4 2
      1 1 3 1 1 1
```

```
    2   3   1          2   3   1 2   2     2   3   1          2   3   1          2   8   4 2   8
  2   3   1          2   3   1      3   1 3   1 3   1          2   3   1          2   3   1
3   1          2   3   1                    2   3   1          2   3   1          8   8
      2   3   1          2              2   3   1          2   3   1          1 1 3 1 1 1
```

```
4 2      4 2      4 2      4 2      8   8      4 2      8   8
  3 1 3 1 3 1 3 1 3 1 3 1 3 1          3 1 3 1 3 1
3 1 4 2      4 2      4 2      4 2 8   4 2   8 4 2    4 2 8   4 2   8
          1 1 3 1 1 1          1 1 3 1 1 1
```

"NN & OO". *On dirty grey cardboard.*

```
1 3      2 4      2 4      2 4      2 4      2 4      2 4      2 4        KEY
      1 3 1 3      1 3 1 3      1 3 1 3      1 3                          X   X
2 4 2 4      1 3 1 3      1 3 1 3      1 3 1 3                            X   X
    1 3      2 4      2 4      2 4      2 4      2 4      2 4             O   O
                                                                        O   O
```

77. Right to left, standard, condensed #3. In the 25th through the 28th columns from the right in the third row, 1 should be on the second row, 2 on the third, 3 on the second, 1 on the bottom, 2 on the second, and 3 on the bottom (instead of all six being on the top two rows). This pattern is similar to Atwater #41, Old Roads.

78. Left to right, condensed #2. The first two columns on the left should be omitted entirely. This is a simple M's & O's draft.

79.
"Guess Me".

```
        3 1 1 3 1           4 2 4 2 3 1              4 2 4 2 3 1
5 3 1 5 3 1 4 2     6 4 2 5 3 1         4 2 4 2 4 2 4 2 3 1
    6 4 2       4 2 5 3 1       3 1     4 2     3 1     3 1     3 1     4 2
6 4 2       2           6 4 2   3 1     3 1     3 1     4 2     3 1
```

80.

```
4  4           4  4         4  4         4  4         4  4         4  4         4  4         4 4
       3  3  3  3         3  3  3  3         3  3  3  3         3  3
2  2  2  2         2  2  2  2         2  2  2  2         2  2  2  2
    1  1         1  1         1  1         1  1         1  1         1  1         1  1
```

81.
"Guinea Foul". *#2 on square cardboard.*

```
2 4   2 4   2 4   2 4   2 4   2 4   2 4   2 4   8   2   8   2 4   8   2   8
1 3   1 3   1 3   1 3   1 3   1 3   1 3   1 3   1   1   1 3   1 3   1 3
8   8   8   8   8   8   8   8   8 8 8 8   8   2 4   2 4
1   1   1   1   1   1   1   1   1 1 1 1 1   1 1   1   1
```

82.
"Guinnie Fowl". *Sun. Sup. 1896.*

```
   2 4      2 4      2 4      2 4      2 4      2 4      2 4      2 4      2 4      2 4 6           2 4 6         2 4 6
   1 3      1 3      1 3      1 3      1 3      1 3      1 3      1 3      1 3              1 3 5 1 3 5 1 3 5
2 4      2 4      2 4      2 4      2 4      2 4      2 4      2 4      2 4      2 4      2 4 6 2 4 6      2 4 6 2 4 6
1 3      1 3      1 3      1 3      1 3      1 3      1 3      1 3      1 3      1 3 1 3 5 1 3 5         1 3 5 1 3 5
```

79. Right to left, historical, condensed #2. In the 32nd and 33rd columns from the right, 2 and 4 should be on the second row up, not the third. The pattern is almost identical to Atwater #66 by the same name.

80. Reads either way, modern notation. Pattern is M's & O's as written, or a small overshot in historical form.

81. Left to right, standard, condensed #3. Similar to Atwater #135, A Patch Pattern from Virginia.

82. Left to right, standard, condensed. Pattern is a wheel with table on opposites.

83.

"Harrysons March". *On brown paper.*

```
1  1  1  1  11  1  1  1  11  1  1  1  11  1  1  1  1
2 2 2 2 2 2 2 2          2 2 2 2 2 2 2 2
  1  1  1  1      1  1  1  1      1  1  1  1      1  1  1  1
        2 2 2 2 2 2 2 2          2 2 2 2 2 2 2 2
```

84.

"Highlanders Delight". *100 years ago, Virginia. Table Linen. 5 Harness.*

```
                           /    /
                     /  /         /  /
  /  /        /  /                    /  /      /  /      /  /      /  /      /  /      /  /
     /  /          /  /                 /  /      /  /      /  /      /  /      /  /
/  /  /  /  /  /  /  /  /  /  /  /  /  /  /  /  /  /  /  /  /  /  /  /  /  /  /  /  /  /  /
```

	Treadling
/ /	3
/ / / /	4
	3
	4
	3
/ / / / /	4
	3
	4
	3
	4
	3
	2
	1
	2
	3
	4
	3
	2
	1
	2

85.

"Honey Comb. Swedish." *Set 20 or 24 splits to the inch. With treadles 1-3 and 2-4 use heavy thread. With treadles 1-2 and 3-4 use fine thread. Treadling: 1-3 and 2-4, heavy thread. 1-2 five times fine. 1-3 and 2-4. 3-4 five times.*

```
                /  /  /  /  /            /  /  /  /  /
             /  /  /  /  /            /  /  /  /  /
  /  /  /  /  /            /  /  /  /  /
/  /  /  /  /            /  /  /  /  /
```

83. Reads either way, standard, condensed #1. This pattern is like Rose #56, but on a finer scale.

84. Right to left, ones. In the final column (left, second line), the bothom line should be one column to the left. This is a spot Bronson weave.

85. Right to left, ones. A simple honeycomb weave.

86.

"Bucien Huckeebuck".

			Tramp
1 3 1 3 1 3 1 3 1 3 1 3 1 3 1 3 1 3			• • • • • • •
2 4 2 4 2 4 2 4			• • • • • • • •
2 4 2 4 2 4			• • • • • • •
2 4 2 4 2 4			

87.

"Indian March". *No date. On an adv. for Brown's Vermiuge Confits or Worm Lozenges. 25 cents a box.*

1 1 1 1 1 11 1 1 1 1 731511 731511 731511 1 1 1 1 11 1 1 1 1
2 2 2 2 2 2 2 2 2 2   6 2   6 2   6 2   6 2   6 2   6 2   2 2 2 2 2 2 2 2 2
1 1 1 1 1   1 1 1 1   5 1   7 3   5 1   7 3   5 1   7 3 1 1 1 1   1 1 1 1 1
2 2 2 2 2 2 2 2 2 8 4   8 8 4 8 8 4   8 8 4 8 8 4   8 8 4 2 2 2 2 2 2 2 2

88.

"Indian War". *On Sun. Suppl. 1896.*

1 11   1   1311   1 731511 731511 731511   1311   1   11 1 1 1 1 1 1 1 1 1
2 2   6 6   6 1   6 2   6 2   6 2   6 2   6 2   6 2   6 6   6 6   2 2   2 2 2 2 2 2 2 2 2
1   1 3 1 1 1   6 1   5 1   7 3   5 1   7 3   5 1   7 3 1 1   1 1 3 1 1   1 1 1 1 1 1 1 1 1
2 2 2   4 2 6 6   4 2   6 6 8 4   6 8 4 6 8 4   6 8 4 6 8 4   6 8 4 6 6   4 2   6 6 4 2   2 2 2 2 2 2 2 2

1 1 1 1 11 1 1
2 2 2 2 2 2 2 2 2
1 1 1 1 1   1 1 1
2 2 2 2 2 2

86. Left to right, condensed #2. The final (right) 2 and 4 should be on the second row up, not the third. A spot Bronson weave.

87. Right to left, standard, condensed #3. This pattern is similar to Burnham #337, with "lozenge lattice".

88. Right to left, standard, condensed #3. This pattern is similar to Atwater #22, Rose of Sharon or Indian War.

89.
"Iowa Draft". *Some one has written "Good for Nothing".*

```
4 2 4 2       4 2 4 2        6 4 2 4 2 4 2 4 2 6 4 2           6 4 2
   3 1 3 1       3 1 3 1          3 1       3 1            3 1    5 3 1
      4 2 4 2       4 2 4 2                   6 4 2 4 2 4 2       6 4 2
3 1      3 1 3 1        3 1 5 3 1     3 1    5 3 1 5 3 1    3 1    5 3 1
```

90.
Sylvia Thomson's Iowa.

```
4 2 4 2       4 2 4 2        6 4 2 4 2 4 2 4 2 6 4 2           6 4 2
   3 1 3 1       3 1 3 1          3 1       3 1          4 2 5 3 1 6 4 2
      4 2 4 2       4 2 4 2                   6 4 2 3 1
3 1      3 1 3 1        3 1 5 3 1     3 1    5 3 1 5 3 1        5 3 1
```

91.
"Irish Chain". *Oldest one.*

```
 1  1  1  1  1  1  1  1  1  1  1  1  1  1  1  1  1  1  1  1  1  1  1  1  1  1  1   1 2 2
 3  3  3  3  3  3  3  3  3  1  1  1  1  1  3  3  3  3  3  3  3  3  3  3  3  3  3 1    2
                                                                             2
 3 1 3 1 3 1 3 1 3 1 3 1 3 1 3 1 3 1 3 1 1 1 1 1 1 1 1 1 1 1 3 1 3 1 3 1 3 1 3 1 3 1 3 1 3 1 3 1 3 1 3 1 3 1 1   2 2
```

```
1   2 2 1         1 2 2  1   2 2 1         1 2 2  1   2 2 1
   2        1 2 2 2 1  2   2   2   2  1 2 2 2 1     2   2       1
      2   2 2                   2   2   2         2
1 2 2  1 1  2  1 1  2 2 1 2 2  1 1  2  1 1  2 2 1 2 2  1 1
```

---

89. Right to left, standard, condensed #2. The pattern is an imperfect Cat Track & Snail Trail type.

90. Right to left, standard, condensed #2. The first 2, 4, 6 on the right should be on the second row up or on the top row, not on the third. The pattern is a slight modification of #89.

91. Left to right, historical, stacked. In the 12th and 18th columns from the left on the second line, both 2s that are on the third row should be on the second row. The pattern is similar to Atwater #47 and #89, Queen's Fancy and Irish Chain.

92.
"IsaaCs Favorite". *On brown paper. Can use 8 instead of 6.*

```
6 4 2    4 2    4 2    4 2    4 2    4 2    4 2    4 2    4 2    4 2    6 6    4 2    6
5 3 1 3 1 3 1 3 1 3 1 3 1 3 1 3 1 3 1 3 1 3 1 3 1 3 1 3 1 3 1 3 1 3 1 3 1 3 1 3 1 1      3 1
     4 2    4 2    4 2    4 2    4 2    4 2    4 2    4 2    4 2    4 2    6      6
                                                                    1 1      1 1
```

93.
"Isaac's Favorite". *Corrected.*

```
               15                    15                  18                 14
 4      4      4  4  4  4  4  4  4  4                 4  4              4  4  4  4  4  4  4
3  3  3  3  3                                         3
   2      2                    2  2  2  2  2  2     2  2  2  2  2  2  2
          1  1  1  1  1  1  1  1  1  1  1  1  1  1  1     1  1  1  1  1  1  1  1  1  1  1  1  1  1
```

```
               14                              51
X X      X      4  4  4  4  4  4  4     4     4     4     4     4     4     4     4     4     4
X        X X   3  3  3  3  3  3  3  3  3  3  3  3  3  3  3  3  3  3  3  3  3  3  3  3  3  3  3
  X  X X                    2     2     2     2     2     2     2     2     2     2     2
X  X X
```

In order to make table effective use an even number of picks in each unit of figure.

```
 /                Tabby
   /
  12
    12
       2
    12
    12
          12
       2
          2
       2
          2
       2
          2
       2
          2
       2
          2
       2
          2
       2
          2
       2
          2
       2
          2
       2
          12
Repeat.
```

---

92. Right to left, standard, condensed #3. This pattern is almost identical to Rose #30 and #67.

93. This appears to be a standard, modern corrected version of #92.

94.
"Jayes Fancy". *On cardboard.*

```
  2 4     2 4     2 4       2 4 6 8   2 4 6 8     2 4       2 4 6 8   2 4 6 8       2 4
              1 3 5 7 1 3 5 7   1 3 5 7                 1 3 5 7 1 3 5 7 1 3 1 3 5 7 1 3 5 7
2 4     2 4     2 4     2 4 6 8       2 4       2 4 6 8   2 4 2 4 6 8       2 4       2 4 6 8
1 3 1 3 1 3 1 3 1 3 1 3         1 3       1 3 5 7 1 3 1 3                               1 3
```

95.
"Jayes Fancey". *1789. On small piece of brown paper.*

```
  2 4     2 4     2 4 8     8   8       8   2 4
              1 1 1 3 1 1 1 1 3 1 1 1 1
2 4     2 4       2 4     8   2 4   8   2 4   8
1 3 1 3 1 3 1 3 1 3 1 3                     1 3
```

96.
"Modified M&O".

```
    4   4       4   4       4   4       4   4       4   4       4   4       4   4
  3   3       3   3       3   3       3   3 3   3       3   3       3   3
    2   2   2   2       2   2       2   2       2   2       2   2       2   2
  1   1       1   1       1   1       1   1       1   1       1   1       1   1
```

```
    4   4       4   4       4   4       4   4       4   4       4   4       4   4
              3   3       3   3   3   3       3   3   3   3       3   3
  2   2   2   2       2   2       2   2   2   2       2   2   2   2
      1   1       1   1       1   1       1   1       1   1       1   1
```

Tread.
3-4
2-3
3-4
1-4
1-2
2-3
1-4
3-4
2-3
3-4
1-4
3-4
1-2
3-4
1-2

94. Left to right, standard, condensed #2. Same as Rose #221.

95. Left to right, standard, condensed #3. Not the same as Rose #94 and #221. This is a double star and table pattern.

96. Left to right, standard, modern. The first (left) four threads of the second line (2, 4, 2, 4) should be omitted—they make an eight-thread cord whereas all the others are four-thread. The pattern is M's & O's.

97.
"THE · KINGS · PUZZEL". *Back of adv. for bread flour.*

```
2   3 4 6     6     6 6     2  2        6   6 6 6     6 2 4 2
2        6 6  6 6     2 4  2  2 2 4   6        6 6             2
  1 1 2    1     1 1   1 3  1  1 1 3 1 1 1   1 1      1 3    1
1      1 1  1 1     1    1 1            1      1 1     1
```

98.
"Ladies Delight". *Long draft.*

```
  4   4   4       4             4   4   4           4   4   4         4   4   4             4     4   4   4   4   4
      3       3                                                                   3       3
          2       2   2   2   2           2   2   2           2   2   2           2   2   2   2       2
1   1   1       1       1   1   1   1   1   1   1   1   1   1   1   1   1   1   1   1   1   1   1       1       1   1   1   1
```

```
  4       4       4   4   4   4   4   4           4   4   4   4   4       4       4       4       4       4       4   4   4
3   3   3   3   3   3                       3       3               3   3   3   3   3   3   3   3   3   3   3   3   3   3   3   3
      2       2                       2   2               2       2       2       2       2       2       2
              1   1   1   1   1       1       1   1   1   1                                                                       1
```

```
  4   4           4   4   4           4   4   4           4       4   4   4   4   4       4       4       4       4
                                                              3       3           3   3   3   3   3   3   3   3   3
      2   2   2           2   2   2           2   2   2   2       2               2       2       2       2       2
1   1   1   1   1   1   1   1   1   1   1   1   1   1   1   1   1       1       1   1   1   1
```

```
  4       4   4   4   4   4   4       4                   4
3   3                       3       3
2   2                   2       2   2   2   2
    1       1   1   1   1   1       1       1   1   1   1
```

97. Left to right, historical, condensed #3. In the third and fourth columns from the left, the 3 and 2 are transposed. The pattern is a fractured wheel.

98. Right to left, standard, modern. The final (left) 16 threads are redundant. This pattern is not like Atwater #137, Ladies Delight, which is a sunflower pattern. It is almost identical to Atwater #19 and #19B, the White Mountain coverlet and its alternate treadling.

99.
"Lady's Fancy #2". *On brown paper.*

```
3 7 6   2     1   1   1   1   1   1   1   1   1   1   1   36   4   1   1   376   4 3 7 6   4   1   1   376
2 6   1   3 2 2 2 2 2 2 2 2 2 2 2 2 2 2 2 2 2 2 2 2 2   2     1 5       2 6   1 5 2 6   1 5       2 6       2
1 5       1   1   1   1   1   1   1   1   1   1   1     1 2 6 1   1   1 1 5   2 6 1 5   2 6 1   1   1 1 5   1   3
  4 1                                               3 7 6 6 6 6 6   4 1 3 7   4 1 3 7 6 6 6 6 6   4 1
```

```
  1   1   1   1   1   1   1   1   1   1   1   36   4
2 2 2 2 2 2 2 2 2 2 2 2 2 2 2 2 2 2 2 2 2 2   2     1 5
1   1   1   1   1   1   1   1   1   1   1           2 6
                                                 1 3 7
```

100.
"Lady's Delight #2". *Sun Sup. 1896.*

```
    1   2       1   2           8   88       1   2       1   2       1   2       8   8   8   8   8       1   2
                    1       1 1                                           1 1 1 1 1 1 1 1 1 1 1 1   2
  2           1   2       1   2 8   8       8 1   2       1   2       1   2       1   2 8   8   8   8   8   2   1           1
1   1   1       1   1   1       1 1 1       1   1   1   1   1   1   1
```

101.
"Lady's Quilt". *1754, Virginia. This is a lovely pattern; would make a nice sofa pillow or coverlet. (Probably from Mrs. Allen.)*

Treadle	or
2-4	1-3
2-3	2-3
2-4	1-3
1-4	1-4
1-3	2-4
2-4	2-3
1-4	1-3
1-3	1-4
2-3	2-4
1-3	2-3
1-4	2-4
2-4	1-3
1-4	2-3
1-3	1-3
2-4	1-4
	2-3
	2-3

```
  1 1     1 1           1 1     1 1   1
1     1 1     1 1 1 1 1     1 1     1
4 4     4 4     4   4     4 4     4 4 4
    4 4     4 4   4   4 4     4 4
```

---

99. Left to right, standard, condensed #2. In the 31st column from the left, the 1 that is on the second row should be on the lowest row. At the right end of the first line, the 1, 2 and 3 that are in columns 57-59 should each be one row higher in the third, top and third rows. This pattern is almost identical to Rose #98, and the same identifications apply.

100. Left to right, standard, condensed #3. In the 44th column from the left, the 1 on the second row should be on the lowest row. The three threads to the left of that block in columns 42 and 43 should also each be one row lower. The pattern is not the same as Rose #98. It is related to Atwater #49.

101. Reads either way, historical, condensed #1. Same as Rose #128. Related to Atwater #34A, Solomon's Delight.

102.
"Ladey Washingtons Delight". *On soiled brown paper, also Sun. Sup. 1896.*

```
1 1   1 1 1   1 1   1   1   1   1   1   1   1   1 1   1 1 1   1 1 1
2       4       2 6 2 6 2 6 2 6 2 6 2 6 2 6 2 6 2       4       2
  1       1     1   1   1   1   1   1   1   1   1       1       1
  2 6 6   6 6 2                             2 6 6   6 6 2   2
```

103.
"Washingtons Delight". *On brown paper.*

```
4 4 4 4 4 4 4 4 4 4   6 6     6 6   4 4 4   4 4 4   4 4 4   4 4 4   4 4 4   4 4 4   4 4 4   4 4 4   4 4 4   4 4 4   6 6       6 6
1   1   1   1   1     1 1     1     1 1 1   1 1 1   1 1 1   1 1 1   1 1 1   1 1 1   1 1 1   1 1 1   1 1 1   1 1 1   1         1 1
                6 6     6 6 6   8       8       8       8       8       8       8       8       8       6       6 6 6     6 6
1   1   1   1   1   1 1     1 1   1 1       1       1       1       1       1       1       1       1       1       1 1   1 1   1
```

```
4 4 4 4 4 4 4 4 4 4 4 4
  1   1   1   1   1   1
```

```
  1   1   1   1   1   1
```

104.
"Leaf and Snow Balls". *Written above is "Good for Nothing".*

```
  2 4       2 4     2 4 2 4         2 4 6 2 4 6       2 4 2 4       2 4       2 4       2 4 2 4         2 4 6 2 4 6     2 4 2 4
1 3       1 3     1 3 1 3       1 3 1 3 5       1 3 1 3         1 3       1 3       1 3       1 3 1 3         1 3 5 1 3     1 3
2 4       2 4     2 4         2 4 2 4       2 4 6 2 4         2 4 2 4       2 4     2 4 1 3       2 4 2 4 6       2 4
  1 3       1 3     1 3 1 3       1 3 5 1 3 5       1 3 1 3       1 3       1 3     2 4 1 3         1 3 5 1 3 5         1 3
```

```
  2 4       2 4     2 4 2 4 6       2 4       2 4 6 2 4       2 4       2 4       2 4 6 2 4       2 4 2 4       2 4       2 4 6 2 4       2 4
1 3       1 3       1 3       1 3 5 1 3 5 1 3 1 3 5 1 3 5       1 3 5 1 3 1 3 5 1 3 5       1 3 1 3 5 1 3 1 3 5 1 3 5
2 4       2 4     2 4         2 4 6       2 4 6         2 4     2 4 6       2 4 6         2 4     2 4 6       2 4 6         2 4
  1 3       1 3     1 3           1 3 1 3 1 3         1 3 1 3 1 3         1 3 1 3 1 3
```

```
2 4 6         2 4 6 2 4     2 4 2 4 6         2 4       2 4 6 2 4       2 4
1 3 5 1 3 5 1 3 5         1 3 5 1 3 5 1 3 1 3 5 1 3 5
    2 4 6         2 4       2 4 6     2 4 6         2 4
        1 3 1 3 1 3         1 3 1 3 1 3
```

---

102. Reads either way, standard, condensed #1. A small Double Chariot Wheel and Table.

103. Reads either way, standard, condensed #1. See Rose #26.

104. Left to right, standard, condensed #2. This draft is full of errors, and has some of the same errors as Atwater #116, Snowball and Leaf. When corrected, both are similar to the design known as Lee's Surrender, a table of stars with a bowknot border.

105.
"Leopard Spots". *Sun. Sup. 1896.*

```
 1 3 5 7             1 3 5 7             1 3 5 7        1 3 5   1 3 5   1 3 5   1 3 5   1 3 5   1 3 5
1 3 5 2 4 6 8 1 3 5       1 3 5 2 4 6 8 1 3 5       1 3 5 2 4 6 8 1 3 5    1 3     1 3     1 3     1 3     1 3     1 3 5
2 4 6       2 4 6 1 3 5 7 2 4 6       2 4 6 1 3 5 7 2 4 6       2 4 6     2 4     2 4     2 4     2 4     2 4     2 4 6
        2 4 6 8                  2 4 6 8              2 4 6   2 4 6   2 4 6   2 4 6   2 4 6   2 4 6
```

```
2 4 6 8             2 4 6 8             2 4 6 8    1 3 5   1   1   1   1   1   1
1 3 5 7 1 3 5       1 3 5 1 3 5 7 1 3 5       1 3 5 1 3 5 7 1 3 5    2 4   2 4   2 4   2 4   2 4   2 4
    2 4 6 2 4 6 8 2 4 6       2 4 6 2 4 6 8 2 4 6       2 4 6    1 3   1 3   1 3   1 3   1 3   1 3
        1 3 5 7                  1 3 5 7              2 4 6   6   6   6   6   6
```

106.
"Lilly of the Valley". *Fairly recent.*

```
 1   1   1   1   1          3 1 1        1 3 1        3 1 1        1 3 1        3 1 1        1 3 1
                     6 4 2       2 6 4 2 2      6 4 2      2 6 4 2 2      6 4 2      2 6 4 2 2      6 4 2
1   1   1   1   1   1 5 3 1 1       5 3 1      5 3 1 1      5 3 1      1 5 3 1 1      5 3 1      1 5 3 1
2 2 2 2 2 2 2 2 2 2       2 4 2      4 2      2 4 2      4 2 2      2 4 2      4 2 2
```

```
        3 1 1        1 3 1        1   1   1   1   1   1   1   1        3 1 1        1 3 1        1   1   1   1   1
3 1   6 4 2       2 6 4 2 2      6 4 2                          6 4 2       2 6 4 2 2      6 4 2
   1 5 3 1 1       5 3 1      1 5 3 1 1   1   1   1   1   1   1   1   1 5 3 1 1       5 3 1      1 5 3 1 1   1   1   1
4 2 2       2 4 2      4 2 2      2 2 2 2 2 2 2 2 2 2 2 2 2 2 2 2 2 2       2 4 2      4 2 2      2 2 2 2 2 2 2 2
```

107.
"LILEY – OF – THE – WEST". *Sun. Suppl. 1896. A duplicate copy reads "Their is best 4 threads in this.*

```
                                                                                                                          Tread.
                                                                                                                          1-2
2 4       2 4 6 2 4 6        2 4 2 4        2 4 2 4 6        2 4 6   2 4        2 4 6 2 4        2 4 2 4        2 4 2 4     1-4
            1 3 5 1 3 5        1 3 1 3        1 3 5 1 3 5           1 3 5 1 3 5        1 3 1 3        1 3 1 3             1-2
    2 4        2 4 6 2 4        2 4 2 4        2 4 6 2 4 6        2 4        2 4 6 2 4 6        2 4 2 4        2 4 2 4     2-3
                                                                                                                          3-4
1 3 1 3 1 3 5        1 3 1 3        1 3 1 3        1 3 5 1 3 5 1 3 1 3 1 3 5        1 3 1 3        1 3 1 3        1 3      1-4
                                                                                                                          1-2
                                                                                                                          2-3
                                                                                                                          1-2
                                                                                                                          2-3
                                                                                                                          3-4
        2 4 6 2 4 6     2 4                                                                                               1-4
     1 3 5 1 3 5                                                                                                          1-2
2 4 2 4 6        2 4     2 4                                                                                              1-4
1 3        1 3 5 1 3 1 3 1 3                                                                                              1-2
                                                                                                                          1-4
                                                                                                                          3-4
```

105. Left to right, standard, condensed #3. This draft has very frequent and numerous breaks in the tabby order because alternate blocks in the first half of the draft are inverted. The pattern is related to Atwater #128, Leopard Skin.

106. Right to left, standard, condensed #2. In the final two columns (left end, second line), the 1 and 3 should be on the top row. There are blocks missing at two places in the threading. The pattern is similar to Atwater #20, a flawed Lily of the Valley or Bonaparte's March.

107. Left to right, standard, condensed #2. Similar to Atwater #100, Wheel of Fortune or Cup & Saucer.

108.
"Linen Weave for Tablecloths or Curtains".

	Tread.
	2-4
	1-3
	2-4
	2-3
	1-2
	2-3
	3-4
	1-4
	1-3

```
1 1    1 1    1 1    1 1    1 1    1 1    1 1    1 1    1 1    1 1    1 1    1 1    1 1
    1 1 1 1        1 1 1 1        1 1 1 1        1 1    1 1    1 1 1 1    1 1    1 1
1 1 1 1        1 1 1 1        1 1 1 1        1 1 1 1    1 1    1 1        1 1    1 1    1 1
    1 1    1 1    1 1    1 1    1 1    1 1    1 1    1 1    1 1    1 1    1 1    1 1
```

109.
"Linsey Draft. Floated Work." *On cardboard, much figured on.*

```
1 3        1 3
    1 3 1 3    1 3 1 3
        2 4 2 4 2 4
2 4 2 4            2 4
```

Tread.
1-4
1-3
2-3
2-4
2-4
2-3
1-3
1-4
1-3
2-3

110.
"Little Window Sash". *1896.*

Tread.
1-4
3-4
2-3
1-2
1-4
1-2
2-3
3-4
1-4
2-3
1-4

```
2 4 6    2 4 6    2 4 6    2 4    2 4    2 4
    1 3    1 3    1 3    1 3 5    1 3 5
    2 4    2 4    2 4    2 4 6    2 4 6
1 3 5    1 3 5    1 3 5    1 3    1 3    1 3
```

108. Reads either way, ones. An M's & O's weave.

109. Left to right, historical, condensed #2. The treadling given is a twill treadling. As draw in treadling weaves a small overshot diamond like Atwater #2, Diamond.

110. Left to right, standard or historical, condensed #2. The pattern is a two-block overshot similar to Rose #4 and related to Atwater #124, a Sugar Loaf or Window Sash pattern.

111.
"M&O".

```
4   4         4   4         4   4           4   4     4   4   4   4         4   4                     4   4
         3   3   3   3               3   3   3   3         3   3   3   3               3   3
  2  2  2  2            2   2   2   2              2   2                  2   2   2   2
     1   1         1   1   1   1         1   1         1   1                  1   1         1   1


4   4         4   4         4   4           4   4         4   4                 4   4         4
         3   3   3   3               3   3   3   3              3   3               3   3
  2  2   2  2           2   2   2   2              2   2   2   2         2   2   2   2
     1   1         1   1         1   1         1   1         1   1   1   1         1   1
```

Tread.	or
2-3	1-2
1-4	3-4
1-2	1-3
2-3	1-2
3-4	2-4
1-4	1-2
1-3	1-3
3-4	3-4
1-2	1-3
3-4	1-2
1-2	2-4
3-4	

112.
"M&O". *Jessie Luther, Hospital Street. Anthoneys Upper New Found Land. Care of Dr. Grenfill's Mission.*

```
2 4      2 4      1 3      2 4      1 3          1 3      2 4 1 3    2 4      1 3      1 3      1 3 2 4    1 3      1 3
      1 3 2 4          1 3 2 4          2 4          1 3          1 3 1 3          2 4 2 4    1 3 2 4          2 4
1 3 2 4        2 4 2 4          2 4 2 4      2 4 2 4      2 4 2 4          2 4 2 4          2 4        2 4 2 4
   1 3      1 3      1 3      1 3      1 3 1 3      1 3          1 3      2 4      1 3      1 3      1 3      1 3


1 3      2 4      2 4      2 4      2 4      2 4      2 4      2 4
      1 3 1 3          1 3 1 3          1 3 1 3          1 3
2 4 2 4          1 3 1 3          1 3 1 3          1 3 1 3
   1 3      2 4      2 4      2 4      2 4      2 4      2 4
```

113.
"Magnolia Blossom".

```
2 6  6   6   6   6   6 2   4 4    4 4    6 8    10 10      12 12    10 8    6 6    4 4    4 2    6   6   6
     2   2   2   2   2   2 2    4 4    6 6    8 8      10 12      10      8 8    6 4    4 4    2 2   2   2   2
2 2   2   2   2   2   2 2    4 4    4 6    8 8    10 10      12 10    8 8    6 6    4 4    2 2      2   2   2
   6   6   6   6   6   6   2 4    4 4    6 6    8 10    12 12      10      8 6    4 4    4 4    2 6   6   6


6   6   6    2 4   4 4    6 6    8 10    12 12      10      8 6    4 4    4 4
   2   2   2 2    4    4 6    8 8      10 10      12 10    8 8    6 6    4 4    2 2
   2   2   2 2   4 4    6 6    8 8      10 12      10      8 8    6 4    4 4    2
   6   6   6 2    4    4 4    6 8    10 10      12 12    10 8    6 6    4 4    4 2
```

---

111. Right to left, modern. M's & O's weave.

112. Left to right, standard, condensed #2. M's & O's weave.

113. Reads either way, historical, stacked. A flawed double bowknot pattern.

114.
"Mary Simmon's Coverlet". *In book of Handwoven Coverlets, p. 150. On dirty brown paper.*

```
1  1  1  1  1  1  1  1  1  11  1  11    1  1    11  1  11    1  1    11  1  1
                        6 6 4 6 8    6 6 4 6 8    6 6 4 6 8    6 6 4 8 8    6 6 4 6 8
1  1  1  1  1  1  1  1  1    1  1   11       11    1  1    11  1  11    1  1
4 6 6 6 6 6 6 6 6 6 6 6 6 6 6 6 6 6 6 6 6        4 6    1    4 6        4 6
```

115.
"Missourie *Compromise*". *on clean brown paper.*

```
   1    1  1  1  1  1  1  1    1           1       1  1  1  1  1  1  1
11   11  1  1  1  1  1  1  1  11  11111  11111  11  1  1  1  1  1  1
6  6  6  2  2  2  2  2  2  6  6  6  6  6  6  6  6  6  2  2  2  2  2
   6  6  6  6  6  6  6  6  6  6  6  6  2  6  6  2  6  6  6  6  6  6  6  6
```

116.
"Misorie Draft". *On brown paper.*

```
       1 3 5                1 3 5  1 3 5  1 3 5  1 3 5  1 3 5  1 3 5  1 3 5  1 3 5          1 3 5
1 3 5 7 1 3 5       1 3 5 1 3 5 7    1      1      1      1      1      1      1    1 3 5 7 1 3 5      1 3 5 1 3 5 7 1 1 3 5 7
2 4 6 8       2 4 6       2 4 6 8              2                             2 4 6 8       2 4 6      2 4 6 8   2 4 6 8
       2 4 6       2 4 6       2 4 6 2 2 4 6 2 2 4 6   2 4 6 2 2 4 6 2 2 4 6 2 2 4 6 2 2 4 6       2 4 6       2 4 6     2
```

```
       1 3 5                          1 3 5          1 3 5  1 3 5  1 3 5  1 3 5  1 3 5  1 3 5  1 3 5  1 3 5
1 3 5       1 3 5 1 3 5 7 1 1 3 5 7 1 3 5       1 3 5 1 3 5 7    1      1      1      1      1      1      1
       2 4 6       2 4 6 8  2 4 6 8       2 4 6       2 4 6 8                                2
2 4 6       2 4 6       2       2 4 6       2 4 6   2 4 6 2 2 4 6 2 2 4 6 2 2 4 6   2 4 6 2 2 4 6 2 2 4 6 2 2 4 6
```

117.

```
       1 3 5          1 3 5  1 3 5  1 3 5  1 3 5  1 3 5  1 3 5  1 3 5  1 3 5          1 3 5
1 1 3 5       1 3 5 1    1      1      1      1      1      1      1    1 1 3 5       1 3 5 1 1 1
8       2 4 6       8      2      2      2      2      2      2      8      2 4 6      8 8
   2 4 6       2 4 6  2 4 6  2 4 6  2 4 6  2 4 6  2 4 6  2 4 6  2 4 6  2 4 6  2 4 6       2 4 6  2
```

```
       1 3 5                1 3 5          1 3 5  1 3 5  1 3 5  1 3 5  1 3 5  1 3 5  1 3 5  1 3 5
1 3 5       1 3 5 1 1 1 1 3 5       1 3 5 1    1      1      1      1      1      1      1
   2 4 6       8 8       2 4 6       8      2      2      2      2      2      2
2 4 6       2 4 6  2  2 4 6       2 4 6  2 4 6  2 4 6  2 4 6  2 4 6  2 4 6  2 4 6  2 4 6  2 4 6
```

114. Reads either way, standard, condensed #2. In the 24th column from the right, the 1 on the lowest row should be on the second row up. The pattern is almost the same as Atwater #61, Queen's Delight or Mary Simmons.

115. Reads either way, historical, condensed #2. This and the next two drafts are similar to Atwater #44, Virginia Snowball.

116. Left to right, historical, condensed #2.

117. Left to right, historical, condensed #3. This is the least flawed of the three versions.

118.
"Missouri Trouble—Celebrated". *Aug. 10, 1821.*

```
    4 2 8 4 2        8  8  8  8  8  8  8  8        4 2 8 4 2        8  8  8  8  8  8  8  8        4 2 8 4 2              8
    3 1 3 1  3 1 3 1                           3 1 3 1  3 1 3 1   1  1  1  1     3 1 3 1  3 1 3 1
  4 2 4 2      4 2 4 2  2  2  2  2  2  2  4 2 4 2      4 2 4 2  2  2  2  2  2  2  4 2 4 2        4 2 4 2
  3 1     1     3 1 1 1 1 1 1 1 1 1 1 1 1 1 1 1 1 3 1       1      3 1 1  1  1  1  1 1 1 1 1 1 1 3 1         1        3 1 1
```

```
8     4 2    8 4 2 4 2 4 2 4 2 4 2 4 2 8    4 2    8 4 2 4 2 4 2 4 2 4 2 4 2 8    4 2    8 8
1 1        1 1    3 1    3 1    3 1    1 1        1 1    3 1    3 1    3 1    1 1        1 1
   8 8    8 8                      8 8    8 8                      8 8    8 8
   1 3 1 1    3 1    3 1    3 1    3 1    1 3 1 1    3 1    3 1    3 1    3 1    1 3 1 1    1
```

119.
On dirty brown paper.

```
  5 2 2 2 2 2 2 5    2    5 5    2 4 2    4  4  4  4  4  4  4  4    2 4 2    4  4  4  4  4  4  4  4    2 4 2    4
  5 5   2  2  2  5 5      5 5    2 2  2 2                      2 2  2 2                      2 2  2 2
5 5              5 5  5 5    2 2    2 2  1 1 1 1 1 1 1 1  2 2    2 2  1 1 1 1 1 1 1 1  2 2    2 2
5    2  2  2  2    5 2 5    5 2    4    2 4 1 4 1 4 1 4 1 4 1 4 1 4 2    4    2 4 1 4 1 4 1 4 1 4 1 4 1 4 2    4    2 4
```

```
5    2    5 2 2 2 2 2 2 5    2
5 5      5 5  2  2  2  5 5
   5 5  5 5              5 5
   5 2 5    2  2  2  2    5 2
```

118. Right to left, standard, condensed #3. A flawed version of #119.

119. Reads either way, standard, stacked. These two drafts are like Atwater #54, Tennessee Trouble (which has a divided table like these; Atwater #53, Missouri Trouble, has a solid table).

120.
"The Morning Star". *Sun. Suppl. 1896.*

```
                                      246246246  246246246      246      246 246246
 135     135     135     135     135     135135     1351135     13513  13135     1351135
 246242462424624242462424624246          2          242424     246    2
    13      13      13      13      13          135          135       13     135          135
```

```
 246     246     246     246     246     246     246     24     24     24     246     246     246
 135131351313135     135131313135     13513133135                         13513133135     13513
    24      24      246      24      246      24      246     246     246     246      24     246      24
          135          135          135131351313513513135          135
```

```
 246     246     246
 135     13513133135
    246      24
    135
```

121.
"Mount Vernon". *On wrapping paper.*

```
 4444444444   66      66  444  444  444  444  444  444  444  444  444  444  66      66
  1  1  1  1  1  11      1   111  111  111  111  111  111  111  111  111  111   1      11
          66     666   6     6    6     6    6    6    6    6    6    6   666     66
  1  1  1  1  11   11  11    1     1    1    1    1    1    1    1    1     11  11    1
```

122.

```
 6     66  222   222   222   222   222   222   222   222   222   222  66     66
    3     662  2102  2102  2102  2102  2102  2102  2102  2102  266     3     66
 636    6     10     10     10    10    10    10    10    10     6   636    66
 66  66     2     2     2    2     2    2    2    2     2   66   66     6
```

```
 2222222222222222222222222222   6
 2  2  2  2  2  2  2  2  2  2  2  2  66
                                   66
 2  2  2  2  2  2  2  2  2  2  2  26
```

---

120. Left to right, standard, condensed #2. An uncorrected version of Rose #19. Similar to Atwater #127 and 1130, Cloudless Beauty and Missouri Check.

121. Reads either way, standard, condensed #1. Both this draft and the next one should have a "D" block added at the end to balance.

122. Reads either way, standard, stacked.

123.
No Name. *Possibly Newport Draft.*

```
1  7        2  1  5        2  1  3        1  1  7  2        2  1  3
   1  7        2  1  5        2  1  3     2        1     2  1  3
      2  1  7        2  1  5        2  1  3  1     2     2  1  3
1        1  7  4  5        2  1  3        2     2  2  1  1  3        2
```

```
         2  1  5        2
      2  1  5        2  1  7
   2  1  5        2  1  7
1  5           2  1  7
```

124.
"NoAh Favorite". *Back of ad for Educator Shoes.*

```
1  31  1     3131    3131        31     31     31     3131    3131    31     31  6  1     31  1
   1     1  31        31        3131    31     31     3131        31        42     31     1  1  31     31  6
         4242        4242              4242           4231              6642424261
664266        424242        424242424242424242        424242        42424261
```

125.

```
3131    3131        31     31     31     3131    3131    31     31     642    531    31     531
   31        3131    31     31     3131        31        42     31     531    531        31     31     642
42        4242              4242        4231                    642642424242642531
   424242        42424242424242424242        424242        424242642531
```

```
531    31     531
   531    531    31
                 42
6426424242642642
```

126.
"Noahs". *Soiled cardboard.*

```
1  1  1  11  11     1  1  1     41  41  1  1  642  1     21     1
   6  6  1     1     11  1  1  11     1     1  1  1        1  31     31  1
      1  44        44              41     44              8842424288
614  6     444        4444444     441     6646531
```

---

123. Left to right, standard, condensed #1. This pattern is a radiating type.

124. Right to left, historical, condensed #3. Variant of the Cross Compass. This draft and #125 and #126 are all slightly flawed versions of the same design.

125. Right to left, historical, condensed #2.

126. Right to left, historical, condensed #3.

127.
"Shuckeroon's Fancy". *See #201.*

```
      4   4   4           4   4   4           4   4   4   4   4                   4   4                   4   4   4   4
  3   3   3           3   3   3           3   3   3   3   3           3   3   3   3           3   3   3   3
  2   2               2   2   2   2   2           2   2   2           2   2   2   2       2   2   2   2
          1   1   1           1   1   1                   1   1               1   1   1   1   1   1           1   1
```

```
  4   4   4   4   4   4           4   4       4   4   4   4   4   4   4                   4   4           4   4   4   4   4
  3   3   3           3   3   3   3   3   3   3   3   3           3   3   3   3                   3   3   3   3           3   3
  2                           2   2               2                   2   2   2   2       2   2   2   2                       2
          1   1               1   1                       1   1           1   1   1   1   1   1           1   1
```

```
  4               4   4                   4   4   4   4   4           4   4   4   4   4   4               4   4
          3   3   3   3   3   3           3   3   3   3       3   3   3   3                                   3
      2   2           2   2   2   2   2   2           2   2   2   2               2   2   2   2           2   2   2
  1   1   1   1   1   1   1   1           1   1   1   1           1   1           1   1       1   1   1   1   1
```

```
  4   4   4               4   4               4
  3   3   3   3   3   3
              2   2   2   2   2   2       2   2
              1   1   1   1   1   1   1   1
```

128.
No name. *On old cardboard.*

```
      3 1 3 1         3 1 3 1               3 1 3 1           3 1 3 1       3 1
  3 1           3 1 3 1           3 1 3 1 3 1 3 1           3 1               3 1
  4 2 4 2           4 2 4 2           4 2       4 2 3 1       4 2 4 2 3 1       4 2 4 2 4 2
          4 2 4 2           4 2 4 2       4 2       4 2 4 2           4 2 4 2
```

127. Right to left, standard, modern. This is a very flawed pattern that contains elements of diamonds, a wheel, and a table, but is incoherent.

128. Right to left, historical, condensed #2. In the ninth and tenth, and 17th and 18th columns, the 3s and 1s should be on the third row up, not the second. The pattern is the same as Rose #101, related to Atwater #34A, Solomon's Delight.

129.
"Number 3" (?). *Sun. Suppl. 1896.*

```
6 4 2 6 4 2 6 4 2 6 4 2        6 4 2        6 4 2 6 4 2 6 4 2 6 4 2 6 4 2        6 4 2          6 4 2            6 4 2            6 4 2
5 3 1        5 3 1        6 4 2        6 4 2      5 3 1        5 3 1          5 3 1      6 4 2        6 4 2        5 3 1        4 2          4 2
              5 3 1        5 3 1                          6 4 2      6 4 2 5 3 1        5 3 1 6 4 2        6 4 2 3 1        3 1
    5 3 1        5 3 1        5 3 1        5 3 1        5 3 1        5 3 1 5 3 1        5 3 1        5 3 1        5 3 1        5 3 1        5 3 1
```

```
                                              6 4 2
    4 2        4 2        4 2        4 2        4 2        4 2      3 1
4 2 3 1 4 2 3 1 4 2 3 1 4 2 3 1 4 2 3 1 4 2 3 1 4 2 4 2 4 2
3 1        3 1        3 1        3 1        3 1        3 1        3 1      3 1 5 3 1
```

130.
"Number 2". *On Sun. Suppl. 1896.*

```
                      4 2 4 2      6      6      4 2 6 6 6 6 6 6 6 6 6 6 6 6 4 2      6      4 2      4 2 4 2
    1      1      1              3 1 1 1 1 1 1 3 1    1    1    1    1    1    1    3 1 1 1 1 3 1 1 3 1
4 2 6 6 6 6 6 4 2              6      6      6                              6      6      6
3 1      1      1      3 1 3 1              1      1      1      1      1      1      1                              3 1
```

131.
No name.

```
2 4 2 4              1 3 1 3 1 3              1 3            2 4 2 4 2 4              2 4
1 3              2 4 2 4      2 4 2 4                    1 3 1 3        1 3 1 3          1    1    1
        1 3 1 3              1 3 1 3      2 4 2 4                2 4 2 4      2 2 2 2 2 2
    1 3 2 4              2 4              2 4 2 4 1 3              1 3              1 3 1 3      1    1    1
```

Tread.

1-2	2-4	3-4
2-3	3-4	2-3
1-2	2-3	1-2
1-4	1-2	1-4
1-2	1-4	
2-3	1-2	
3-4	2-3	

---

129. Right to left, standard, condensed #2. There are many breaks in the tabby order because almost all of the blocks onthe middle shafts are inverted. Pattern is similar to Rose #132.

130. Right to left, standard, condensed #3. Similar to Rose #191, #192 and #195. Similar to Atwater #137 and #141. Pattern is a single Sunflower.

131. Left to right, standard, condensed #2. Pattern is a divided diamond design.

132.
No name. 282 threads.

```
   5 3 1     5 3 1     5 3 1     5 3 1     5 3 1     5 3 1     5 3 1     5 3 1     5 3 1     5 3 1     5 3 1
6 4 2 6 4 2 6 4 2 6 4 2 6 4 2 6 4 2 6 4 2 6 4 2 6 4 2 6 4 2 6 4 2 6 4 2 6 4 2 6 4 2 6 4 2 6 4 2 6 4 2 6 4 2 6 4 2 6 4 2 6 4 2 6 4 2 6 4 2 6 4 2 6 4 2 6 4 2
5 3 1     5 3 1     5 3 1     5 3 1     5 3 1     5 3 1     5 3 1     5 3 1     5 3 1     5 3 1     5 3 1     5 3 1
```

```
6 4 2           6 4 2           6 4 2 6 4 2           6 4 2 6 4 2 6 4 2 6 4 2 6 4 2 6 4 2 6 4 2 6 4 2 6 4 2 6 4 2           6 4 2
5 3 1     5 3 1    ·5 3 1     5 3 1     5 3 1     5 3 1     5 3 1     5 3 1     5 3 1     5 3 1     5 3 1     5 3 1
    6 4 2 6 4 2     6 4 2 6 4 2           6 4 2 6 4 2                          6 4 2 6 4 2
    5 3 1     5 3 1     5 3 1     5 3 1     5 3 1     5 3 1     5 3 1     5 3 1     5 3 1     5 3 1     5 3 1     5 3 1
```

133.
No name.

```
      1 4 2 3 1 3 1 3 1 1 1 1 1 1      1    1    1 1                                                          1
8         3 1    4 2    2    6      1   2 2 2 8      3 1      3 1      3 1      3 1      3 1      4 2
1 3 1                          4 2 6    1    1      4 2 4 2 4 2 4 2 4 2 4 2 4 2 4 2 4 2 4 2 4 2 3 1 1
    4 2 8    4 2    4 2   6    6 3 1   2        2 3 1      3 1      3 1      3 1      3 1      3 1      6 6
```

134.
No name.

```
1 3 5 7             2    1    3          2 4   1 3 5          2 4 6   1 3 5 7
        2         2 1    3             2 4   1 3 5          2 4 6   1 3 5 7       1 3
    2 1   2    1    3          2 4   1 3 5          2 4 6   1 3 5 7          2 4
2 4 6   1   1    3          2   1 3 5          2 4   1 3 5 7          2 4 6
```

```
2 2 2 2 2 2 2 2 2 2 2 2 2 2 2 2 2    2 4 6
1   1   1   1   1   1   1   1   1   1 3          1 3
                               2 4          2 4
  1   1   1   1   1   1   1   1    1 3 5 7
```

```
2 4     2 4 6      1 3     1 3 5 7    2 2 2 2 2 2 2 2 2 2 2 2 2 2 2      1 1   7          2 4   1   5
    1 3          2 4    2 4          2 4 1 1 1 1 1 1 1 1 1 3 5    2    1    7               2
    2 4          1 3    1 3          1 3                      2 4          2    1    7
1 3     1 3 5 7    2 4     2 4 6 8      1   1   1   1   1   1   1      8             2    1    5
```

132. Left to right, standard, condensed #2. Pattern begins on lowest shaft; the entire first line uses only the lower three shafts. Design is similar to Rose #129.

133. Right to left, standard, condensed #3. Identical to Rose #215. A flawed version of Atwater #145, The Warner Coverlet (a Velvet Rose pattern).

134. Left to right, standard, condensed #3. Error: in 6th column from left, first line, the 1 and 2 should be transposed (the block inverted). This pattern is the same as Rose #196, and related to Atwater #106, Sunrise on the Walls of Troy.

135.
No name.

```
     6      2 6 2      6        6        6        6        6        6        6        4 2 6 4 2 4 2
          1 1      1 1                                                        3 1 3 1      3 1 3 1      6 4 2
2      2 2      2 2      2        2        2        2        2        2        2 4 2      4 2 4 2
  1 5 3 1 1      5 3 1    1 5 3 1    1 5 3 1    1 5 3 1    1 5 3 1    1 5 3 1    1 5 3 1    1 5 3 1 1      5 3 1      3 1 5 3 1
```

```
                                   2 6 2      6        6        6        6        6        6        6
4 2 8                  4 2        8    8    1 1      1 1
    7  17 1                7  17 1      2        2 2      2        2        2        2        2        2
          8    8        8    8        2    5 3 1    1 5 3 1    1 5 3 1    1 5 3 1    1 5 3 1    1 5 3 1    1 5 3 1    1 5 3 1
3 1            7  13 17  1            5 3 1 1
```

136.
No name.

```
   1 3      1 3      1 3      1 3      1 3      1 3      1 3          1 3 1 3        1 3 1 3      1 3 1 3        1 3 4 3        2 4 1 3
                                                    2 4 2 4        2 4 2 4        2 4 2 4 2 4        2 4 2 4        1 3 1 3            1 3
1 3      1 3      1 3      1 3      1 3      1 3      1 3      1 3 1 3        1 3 1 3              1 3        1 3 1 3        2 4 2 4        2 4 2 4
2 4 2 4 2 4 2 4 2 4 2 4 2 4 2 4 2 4 2 4 2 4 2 4 2 4 2 4 2 4 2 4        2 4 2 4          2 4 2 4            2 4 2 4        2 4 1 3        2 4 1 3
```

```
2 4 2 4          2 4        2 4 2 4
1 3          1 3 1 3 1 3        1 3 1 3        1 3
      2 4 2 4      2 4 2 4          2 4 2 4 2 4
   1 3 1 3          1 3 1 3          1 3
```

137.
No name.

```
1 3 1 3        1 3 1 3        1 3 1 3        1 3 5 1 1 1 1          1 3 5
    2 4 2 4        2 4 2 4        2 4 2 4            6    6      6  2 4 6 2 4 6
        1 3 1 3        1 3 1 3        1 3 1 3              1 3 5 1 1        1 3 5
2 4          2 4 2 4          2 4 2 4          2 4 2 4 6  2  6 2 4 6  2
```

---

135. Right to left, standard, condensed #3. Errors: in the first line, the first 2, 4, 6 should be on the top row, not the third. The 6's in columns 19, 24, 29, 34, 39, 44, 49, 54, 60 and 66 should each be moved one column to the left, as should the similar 6's in the second line. In the second line, the entire first section of 41 columns should be moved down one row.

136. Left to right, standard, condensed #2. This pattern is the same as Rose #228, and is a flawed diamond and table design.

137. Left to right, standard, condensed #3. Identical to Rose #205. Similar to Atwater #38, an imperfect Cat Track and Snail Trail type.

138.
No name.

```
4  4  4  4  4  4  4  4  4  4  4  4  4  4  4  4  4  4  4  4  4  4  4              4  4  4
         3     3  3  3  3  3     3  3  3  3  3     3              3  3  3        3  3  3
                                                       2  2  2  2  2  2            2  2
1  1  1  1     1              1        1  1  1  1  1  1           1  1  1              1
```

```
                  4  4  4              4  4  4
3  3     3  3  3        3  3  3     3  3  3        3  3  3
2  2  2  2  2  2  2  2  2     2  2  2     2  2  2  2
      1        1  1  1  1        1           1  1  1           1
```

139.
No name. (Whig Rose).

```
            4  4  4  4  4  4  4  4  4  4  4  4  4  4  4  4  4  4  4                 4  4  4
3  3                    3     3  3  3  3     3  3  3  3     3              3  3  3        3  3  3
2  2  2  2                                               2  2  2  2  2  2            2  2
      1  1  1  1  1     1                 1              1        1  1  1  1  1           1  1  1              1
```

```
4  4  4  4  4  4  4                          4  4  4              4  4  4
3  3     3              3  3  3        3  3  3        3  3  3        3
         2  2  2  2  2  2        2  2  2     2  2
      1        1  1  1  1  1        1  1  1        1  1  1        1  1  1
```

140.
This has "Nothing" written on it.

```
6 2 4 2 4 6 2 4 2 4 6 2 4 2 4 6 2 4 2 4 6 2 4 2 4 6                   1   3
1      1 3 5      1 3 5      1 3 5      1 3 5      1 3 5 1   3      1   3   2      1 3      1 3      1 3            2
                                                            2   1   3   2        2 4 2 4 2 4 2 4 2 4   2   1   3
   1 3        1 3        1 3        1 3        1 3            2                1 3      1 3      1 3      1  3
```

```
   2   1   3   2                                          2   1   3   2
1  3        1   3   2                                     2   1   3      1   3   2                  1 3
            1   3 1     3 1     3 2 4 2 4 2 4 2 4 2 4   2   1   3              1   3 1     3 2 4 2 4
         2         2     2   1 3      1 3      1 3      1   3      2                 2   1 3
```

```
2 4 2 4 2 4          2 4 2 4 6 2 4 2 4 6 2 4 2 4 6 2 4 2 4 6        2 4 2 4 2 4
      1 3 1 3            1 3 5      1 3 5      1 3 5      1 3 5      1 3 1 3      1 3 1 3
      2 4 2 4                              2 4 2 4              2 4 2 4
1 3 1 3        1 3 1 3        1 3      1 3      1 3      1 3        1 3        1 3
```

138. Reads either way, standard, modern. This pattern and #139 are both flawed versions of a Single Chariot Wheel pattern similar to Atwater #65.

139. Reads either way, standard, modern. This is an imperfect version of #138, and is not the same as Atwater's Whig Rose.

140. Left to right, standard, condensed #3. Flawed alternating divided tables.

141.
No name. *On old piece of pasteboard box. (M&O).*

```
    2 4       2 4       2 4
      1 3       1 3       1 3
  2 4       2 4       2 4
  1 3       1 3       1 3
```
etc.

142.
No name. *On wrapping paper.*

```
      6     6     6     6     6         1  3           2           2  1  3
  2 4 1 1 3 1 1 3 1 1 3 1 1 3 1 1   3  2  1  3           2  1  3              2 4       2 4       2 4
  1 3   2 4   2 4   2 4   2 4   2       2  1  3     1  3          2 4 6     2 4 6     2 4 6
                          2  1  3           2   1 3 5 1 3 1 3 5 1 3 1 3 5 1 3
```

```
              2   1   3   2         2   1   3   2
      2 4       2 4       2   1   3
  2 4 6     2 4 6               1   3
  1 3 5 1 3 1 3 5 1 3 1   3         2   1   3   2   1   3
```

143.
No name. *On wrapping paper.*

```
    6 4 2 4 2   4 2   4 2   3 1   4 2   4 2   4 2   4 2   4 2   4 2   4 2   4 2   4 2
  5 3 1       3 1   3 1   3 1   3 1   3 2   3 1   3 1   3 1   3 1   3 1   3 1   3 1
  6 4 2 5 3 1   4 2   4 2   4 2   4 2   4 1   4 2   4 2   4 2   4 2   4 2   4 2   4 2
        3 1   3 1   3 1   4 2   3 1   3 1   3 1   3 1   3 1   3 1   3 1   3 1   3 1
```

```
        2     2     2         5 3 1 1   1   1   1   1   1   1 5 3 1       2     2     2
  5 3 1     3 1   3 1   3 1   3 1 5 3 1     3 1   3 1   3 1   3 1   3 1   3 1       5 3 1 3 1   3 1   3 1
      5 3 1   1   1   1   6 4 2 6 4 2               4 2       6 4 2 6 4 2   1   1   1
  6 4 2 6 4 2 4 2   4 2   4 2   4 2       8 4 2 8 4 2 8 4 2 8 4 2 8 4 2 8   8 4 2 8       4 2   4 2   4 2
```

---

141. Left to right, condensed #2. The first eight threads constitute one repeat. Marked M's & O's, but uses only one block; could be treated as a small 2-block overshot on opposite blocks.

142. Left to right, standard, condensed #3. Errors: apparently, the 2's and 4's in columns 43, 44, 48, 49, 53 and 54 of the first line and columns 4, 5, 9 and 10 of the second line should all be on the top row instead of third row. Assuming that, this is a flawed pattern of alternating tables.

143. Right to left, historical, condensed #3. There are frequent and numerous breaks in the tabby order in this draft because alternate blocks in the opposite-block tables are inverted. Pattern is a flawed design of alternating tables with a connecting star. It is similar to Rose #10 and #11 and Atwater #82, Arrow.

144.
No name.

```
1  32424           24          24241  3                    2                1  3            1  3                1  3
   2      1324              1313        2  1  3                  1  3  2  1  3                1  3  2
          1324      2424                  2  1  3        1  3  2        2  1  3        1  3  2
      1 3          131313          1 3              2  1  3  2              2      2      2
```

145.
No name. *On cardboard.*

	Repeat		Key

```
     1 3      1313            1313              1313          1 3      1 3      X X
1 3      1 3      2 4      1 3      2 4      1 3      2 4      1 3      1 3      O  O
     2 4      2 4      1 3      2 4      1 3      2 4      1 3      2 4      2 4  X  X
2 4      2 4      2424          2424          2424      2 4                    OO
```

146.
No name.

```
                                                2 4 6 8 10 12
                    2 4        2 4        2 4              246246
2 4 6 8 10 2 4 6 8 10          2 4        2 4      246246
  3    7      1    5    9    3    3    3    3    3    3    1    5    3    1    5    3    7      11
  1    5    9    3    7    1    1    1    1    11    1    1    5    3    1    5    3    1    5    9
```

```
2 4 6 8        2 4 6 8
        2 4        2 4 6 8 10 12
                                246        246        246
                                246        246
  3    7    3    3    7    3    7      11    3      3      3      3      3
  1    5    1    1    5    1    5    9      1      51      51      51      51      5
```

```
              2 4 6 8        2 4 6 8
2 4 6 8 10 12          2 4        2 4 6 8 10 12
                                2 4 6 8 10 12                2 4        2 4        2 4                      2 4
                                    2 4 6 8 10 12    2 4        2 4    2 4 6 8 10 12 14 16 18 20
  3    7      11    3    7    3    3    7    3    7      11    3    7      11    3    7      11    3    3    3    3    3    7      11      15      19    3
  1    5    9      1    5      11    5    1    5    9      1    5    9      1    5    9      1    1    1    1      11    5    9      13      17        1
```

144. Left to right, standard, condensed #2. A flawed variable diamond similar to Atwater #1 and #2, Russian Diaper.

145. Reads either way, condensed #2. Repeat is as marked. Could be M's & O's or a small overshot (with 1-3, 2-4, 1-2 and 3-4 as the pattern blocks and 1-4 vs 2-3 as tabbies).

146. Left to right, condensed #2. Summer & winter weave with 2-thread blocks. Errors: there are five flaws in the pattern where successive 5 and 1 tiedowns fall on the same shaft (first line, 61st through 71st columns). Pattern is the same as Rose #40 in a different scale. See Atwater #196, Mosaics.

· 95 ·

147.
No name. *On rather dirty brown paper.*

```
                              2 4 6 8 10 12 2 4 6 8 10 12 2 4 6 8 10 12
2 4 6 8 10 12 2 4 6 8 10 12 2 4 6 8 10 12

  3    7    11    3    7    11    3    7    11    3    7    11    3    7    11    3    7    11
1    5    9    1    5    9    1    5    9    1    5    9    1    5    9    1    5    9


2 4 6 8 2 4 6 8 2 4 6 8            2 4 6 8 2 4 6 8 2 4 6 8
               2 4 6 8 10 12

  3   7   3   7   3   7   3   7   11   3   7   3   7   3   7
1   5   1   5   1   5   1   5   9   1   5   1   5   1   5
```

148.
No name. *On back of a Tomato Catsup adv. (Barley Corn).*

```
  3 1      3 1              3 1      3 1            3 1          3 1      3 1            3 1      3 1      3 1
3 1      3 1            3 1              3 1                3 1          3 1              3 1      3 1
            3 1              3 1              3 1                3 1                          3 1      3 1      3 1
            3 1              3 1              3 1      3 1              3 1              3 1                3 1      3 1      3 1      3 1
4 2 4 2 4 2 4 2 4 2 4 2 4 2 4 2 4 2 4 2 4 2 4 2 4 2 4 2 4 2 4 2 4 2 4 2 4 2 4 2 4 2 4 2 4 2 4 2 4 2 4 2 4 2 4 2 4 2 4 2 4 2 4 2 4 2 4 2 4 2


                                    3 1
3 1        3 1        3 1        3 1
      3 1        3 1        3 1        3 1
4 2 4 2 4 2 4 2 4 2 4 2 4 2 4 2 4 2 4 2
```

147. Left to right, condensed #2. Three-block summer & winter weave (4-thread blocks). Pattern is a diagonal or an incomplete star.

148. Right to left, condensed #2. Spot Bronson weave. Block design is like Rose #39, a Cross Compass variant.

149.

No name. *Coverlet draft. Draft reads 1 warp thread on first harness, 12 on the 4th, 1 on the 2nd, 12 on the 3rd, etc. Treadles follow the order of threading: 1-4; 2-3; 1-4; 1-3; 2-3; etc.*

1	1		3	3	3	3	3	1	1	3	3	3	3	3	1	1	3	3	3	3	3	1	1
1	1	1	1	1	1	1		1		1	1	1	1		1	1	1	1	1	1		1	
6	12		1	1	1	1	1	12	1 1	1	1	1	1	12		1	1	1	1	1	1	12	
6	12	12 3	3	3	3	3	12	12 3	3	3	3	3	12	12 3	3	3	3	3	12	12			

1	1	1	1	1	1	1	1	1	1	1	1	1	1
1	1	1	1	1	1	1	1	1	1	1	1	1	1	1
6	6	6	6	6	6	6	6	6	6	6	6	6	6	6
6	6	6	6	6	6	6	6	6	6	6	6	6		

150.

No name.

	2 4 6 2 4 6		1 3 5 7	2		1	3	2		2	1 3 5		2 3 5 7 1 3 5 7
	1 3 5 7 2 4 6			1	3	2			2	1	3	2 4 6 1 4 6	
2 4 6		1 3 5 7 2 4 6			1	3	2		1	3		1 3 5 1 3 5 7	
1 3 5 1 3 5		1 3 5 7 2 4 6				1	3	2 1	3		2 4 6 2 4 6		2 4 6

	2 4 6		2 4 6	
	1 3 5			1 3 5
2 4 6 2 4 6		2 4 6		2 4 6 2 4 6
1 3 5		1 3 5 1 3 5 1 3 5		1 3 5

149. Left to right, historical, condensed #2. Errors: in first line the 1 in the 24th column from the left should be on third row, not second. The designation of 1 and 3 for each of the blocks in the three small tables is strange. The pattern is a stars and table on opposites, a Patch type.

150. Left to right, standard, condensed #2. Error: in the 54th to 56th columsn from left, the 3, 4, 5, 6, 7 part of that blocks is inverted. Pattern is a radiating type similar to Star of Bethlehem, but full of errors.

151.

No name. *On a very mussed and dirty piece of wrapping paper. This verse is written on the back:*
Herbert D. Gross is a neat little bean
If I did but have him to the Colidg h'de go
When he gets there he studies repair and
Building new houses by Compass and Square.

```
      1 1      1 3 5 2 4 6   2  1 3 5 1 3 5    2 2    2 4 6
    2 2      2 2 4          1  3      2 4  1      1 1          1  1  1  1  1  1  1  1  1
  2   1    1 1                          2 2      2 2    2 4 2 2 2 2 2 2 2 2 2 2 2 2 2 2 2 2 2 2 3
1   3    2 2          1 3 5      2 4 6      1 1      1 1 3 5 1 3  1  1  1  1  1  1  1  1  1  1  1 4
```

```
                                                                    Tread.
                                                                    1-2
2 4 6      2 2          1 3 5 2 4 6   2  1 3 5 1 3 5    2 2          2-3
        1 1    1  3 2 4          1  3      2 4  1    1 1             3-4
      2 2    2  2                              2 2    2              1-4
1 3 5 1    1 1          1 3 5      2 4 6      1 1                    1-2
                                                                    2-3
                                                                    3-4
                                                                    1-4
                                                                    3-4
                                                                    1-4
                                                                    3-4
                                                                    2-3
                                                                    1-2
                                                                    1-4
                                                                    3-4
                                                                    1-2
                                                                    2-3
                                                                    1-2
                                                                    2-3
                                                                    1-2
                                                                    1-4
                                                                    1-2
                                                                    2-3
```

152.

No name. *"Bad" has been written on it.*

```
      4   4   4   4   4          4   4   4   4   4                4   4   4          4   4   4
  3   3   3   3                    3   3   3   3   3
2 2                    2   2   2              2   2   2   2   2          2   2   2
              1  1  1  1  1  1  1  1  1                  1  1  1  1  1  1  1  1  1  1  1  1  1  1
```

```
      4   4   4                    4   4   4          4   4   4
              3   3   3   3   3   3   3   3   3   3   3   3   3   3   3
2   2   2              2   2   2   2   2              2   2   2              2   2   2
1  1  1  1  1  1  1  1
```

---

151. Left to right, standard, condensed #2. In the first line, the right 3 and 4 are inverted. Treadling is a twill. When woven as drawn in, this pattern is almost identical to Rose #34.

152. Left to right, standard, modern.

153.
No name. *"Bad"*.

```
        6 4 2 6 4 2        6 4 2 6 4 2             6 4 2       6 4 2             6 4 2       6 4 2
     5 3 1 5 3 1             5 3 1 5 3 1                             5 3 1 5 3 1 5 3 1 5 3 1 5 3 1
 6 4 2 6 4 2         6 4 2         6 4 2 6 4 2       6 4 2       5 3 1 6 4 2       6 4 2       6 4 2
 5 3 1         5 3 1 5 3 1 5 3 1             5 3 1 5 3 1 5 3 1 5 3 1 6 4 2
```

```
 6 4 2       6 4 2       6 4 2
 5 3 1 5 3 1 5 3 1 5 3 1 5 3 1 5 3 1       6 4 2       6 4 2
       6 4 2       6 4 2       6 4 2 6 4 2       6 4 2       6 4 2 6 4 2
                         5 3 1 5 3 1 5 3 1 5 3 1 5 3 1 5 3 1
```

Treadle
1-4
1-2
1-4
3-4
2-3
3-4
1-4
1-2
1-4
1-2
1-4
1-2
1-4
3-4
2-3
1-2
1-4
1-2

154.
No Name. Rose Coverlet. *(Very good.)*

```
                              |A
      4   4           4   4       4       4   4       4       4   4           4   4
   3   3   3   3           3   3       3   3       3   3   3   3   3
 2   2   2       2   2   2       2       2       2       2       2   2   2       2   2   2
 1           1   1   1   1       1   1   1       1   1   1   1           1   1
```

```
                    |B
   4       4   4       4       4   4           4   4
   3   3       3   3       3   3   3   3   3
 2       2       2       2       2   2   2       2   2
 1       1   1   1       1   1   1   1       1
```

Tread.
1-2
2-3
3-4
3-2
1-2
1-4
1-2
2-3
3-4
3-2
1-2
1-4
Repeat

155.
No name. Coverlet.

```
      4   4   4   4   4           4   4
 3   3   3   3   3       3   3   3   3   3   3   3
 2   2   2       2   2   2       2   2   2   2   2
      1   1   1   1   1   1   1   1       1   1   1
```

---

153. Right to left, standard, condensed #2. In the first line, sixth block (16th-18th columns) should be inverted. In the second line, the 2, 4 and 6 in the first, third and fifth blocks of that line should all be on the top row, not on the second or third.

154. Right to left, A to B, standard, modern. If the excess draft outside the A to B repeat is used, the final 7 threads (left end, second line) should be moved one thread to the left so that the 1 is not under the 4 in 28th column. Pattern is similar to Rose #156. Treadling given is just point twill repeated twice.

155. Reads either way, standard, modern. The 3's in columns 16-22 should be 2's. Pattern is a fractured semi-diamond or "hammerhead" twill.

156.

No name. Coverlet.

```
        4   4           4   4   4       4       4   4   4       4       4   4   4               4   4
    3   3   3   3   3               3   3               3   3               3   3   3   3   3
2   2   2           2   2   2           2           2           2           2   2   2           2   2   2
    1               1   1   1   1           1   1   1   1           1   1   1   1                   1   1
```

157.

No name. 1896.

```
1 3 5       1       1 3 5 2 4     2 4 1 3 5       1       1 3 5 2 4     2 4 1 3 5       1       1 3 5 1 3
                      1 3 1 3 1 3                           1 3 1 3 1 3                           2 4 2 4
    1 3 5   1 3 5           2 4           1 3 5   1 3 5           2 4           1 3 5   1 3 5           1 3
2 4 6 2 4 6 2 2 4 6 2 4 6               2 4 6 2 4 6 2 2 4 6 2 4 6               2 4 6 2 4 6 2 2 4 6 2 4 6
```

```
1 3         1 3         1 3         1 3         2 4 2 4         2 4 2 4  2 4 2 4         2 4 2 4  2 4 2 4         2 4
2 4 2 4 2 4 2 4 2 4 2 4 2 4 2 4 6       1 3 2 4 6 2 4           6           2 4 6 2 4           6       2 4 6 2 4
    1 3         1 3         1 3         1 3             1 3   1 3 1 3           1 3 1 3   1 3 1 3           1 3 1 3   1 3
                      1 1 3         1           1 3 1 1 3           1       1 3 1 1 3           1       1 3
```

```
    2 4 2 4             2 4 1 3     1 3 2   2 4 6   6       2 4 6       2   2   2 4   2 4 6 2 4           6 2 4 2
6           2 4 6 2 4       2 4 2 4 2 4   2       6   6 6       2 4   2   2   6           2 4 2 4           2
    1 3 1 3   1 3 1 3           1 3           1 1 3   1       1 1 3   1 3   1   1 1 3 1 1 3   1 3 1 3           1 3   1
1 1 3       1                   1           1   1 1     1       1 1       1                   1 3 1       1
```

158.

No name. *On a very dirty pasteboard with blue back.*

```
1 3 1 3           1 3           1 3 1   1   1 1     1 3   1 3   1 3     1 1   1   1 1 3           1 3           1 3 1 3
    1 3 1 3           1 3 1 3     1   1   8 1 3     1       1       1 3     1 1       1 3 1 3       1 3           1 3
    2 4 2 4                   2 4 2 4           2 4 2 4 8 2 4 8 2 4 2 4 8       2 4 2 4           2 4 2 4           2 4
2 4         2 4 2 4 2 4           6 6 2 6 6                   6 6 2 6 6       2 4 2 4           2 4
```

```
    1 3           1 3           1 3           1 3 1 3
1 3         1 3 1 3     1 3 1 3 1 3       1 3 1 3           1 3
                  2 4 2 4     2 4             2 4 2 4
2 4 2 4 2 4           2 4     2 4 2 4 2 4           2 4 2 4
```

156. Reads either way, standard, modern. The treadling given is a point twill. Treadled as drawn in, this pattern is similar to Rose #154.

157. Left to right, standard, condensed #3. The notation style reverts to historical in the second and third lines. To make it weaveable, the upper numbers in any block on first and third rows must be moved down to second row, and the lower numbers in any block on second and fourth rows must be moved up to third row. There are 22 such blocks. Even when these changes are made, the pattenr remains very flawed. It is a compound design of stars, a table, and diamonds.

158. Left to right, historical, condensed #3. Error: in 22nd column from left, first line, the 8 should be on the second row, not third. Pattern is a flawed version of Rose #206 and #220 and of Atwater #79, Lover's Knot.

159.
No name.

```
2 4         2 4         2 4 1 1 1 1 1 1 1 1 1 1 3 5 2 4         2 4 2 4 2 4
    1 3         1 3         1 3 5 2 2 2 2 2 2 2 2 2 2 2 2 2 2 2 2 2 2 2 2 4         1 3 1 3         1 3 1 3
    2 4 2 4         2 4 2 4         1 1 1 1 1 1 1 1 1 1 1         2 4 2 4         2 4 2 4
1 3 1 3         1 3         1 3                                          1 3 1 3         1 3         1 3
```

```
2 4   4 1 3 3 7 2 4   4 1 3 3 7 2 4   4 1 3 3 7 2 4   4 1 3 3 7
    1 5     2 6     1 5     2 6     1 5     2 6     1 5     2 6
    2 6     1 5     2 6     1 5     2 6     1 5     2 6     1 5
1 3 3 7 2 4   4 1 3 3 7 2 4   4 1 3 3 7 2 4   4 1 3 3 7 2 4   4
```

160.
No name. *Evidently used quite a lot.*

```
1         1         1         1         1
2 2   1   3 2   2   1   3 2   2   1   3 2   2   1   3 2   2
    1 2   2   1   3 2   2   1   3 2   2   1   3 2   2   1   3
    1         1         1         1
```

```
    2   3 7   2       1   3   4 1   3       1           1           1           1
        2 6           1           1 5       1   3 2   2   1   3 2   2   1   3 2   2   1   3 2   2
2       1 5       1   3 2   2       2 6       2   2   1   3 2   2   1   3 2   2   1   3 2   2   1   3 2
1 1   3   4 1   3   2   1   3   2   3 7   2   1       1           1           1           1
```

161.

```
    4   4           4   4       4       4   4           4               4               4               4
    3           3           3       3           3 3 3 3       3 3 3 3       3 3 3 3       3 3 3 3
2       2 2 2 2       2       2       2 2       2 2 2 2       2 2 2 2       2 2 2 2       2 2 2
1   1 1 1   1 1 1   1   1 1 1           1           1           1           1
```

```
                4               4               4               4           4 4       4
3 3       3 3 3 3       3 3 3 3       3 3 3 3       3 3 3 3       3
2 2   2 2       2 2 2 2       2 2 2 2       2 2 2 2       2 2       2
        1           1           1           1           1 1 1
```

Tread. #2	Tread. #1	center
2-3	2-3	2-3
1-2	3-4	2-3
1-4	2-3	1-2
3-4	1-2	1-4
1-2	3-2	2-3
1-4	3-4	1-4
3-4	2-3	2-3
2-3	1-2	1-4
1-2	1-4	1-2
1-4	2-3	3-4
1-2	1-4	2-3
2-3	2-3	1-2
3-4	1-4	2-3
2-3	1-2	3-4
1-2	2-3	2-3
2-3		
3-4		

159. Left to right, standard, condensed #2.

160. Left to right, standard, condensed #2. This pattern is a flawed version of Rose #47. See also Rose #213 and #239.

161. Right to left, standard, modern. The treadlings given are point-twill-like.

162.
"Ohio Beauty or Wonder of the Forest". *1834.*

```
8 4 4 4 8 8 8 8 8 8 8 4 4 4 8 8 8 8 8 8 8 8 8 8 8 8 8 8 8 8 8
1         1 1 1   1 1 1   1 1 1           1 1 1   1 1 1 1 1 1 1 1 1 1 1 1 1 1 1 1 1 1 1 1 1 1 1 1 1 1 1 1 1 1 1 1  1 1
8 8 8 8 4 8 4 8 4 8 8 8 8 4 8 4 4 4 4 4 4 4 4 4 4 4 4 4 8 4
1 1 1 1 1 1 1       1       1       1 1 1 1 1 1 1       1                          .                          1
```

163.

```
6 4 4 4 6 6 6 6 6 6 4 4 4 6 6 6 6 6 6 6 6 6 6 6 6 6 6 6
1         1 1 1 1 1 1 1 1 1       1 1 1   1 1 1 1 1 1 1 1 1 1 1 1 1 1 1 1 1 1 1 1 1 1 1 1 1 1 1 1 1 1 1  1 1
4 6 6 6 4 4 6 4 6 6 6 6 4 6 4 4 4 4 4 4 4 4 4 4 4 4 6 4
1 1 1 1 1 1 1             1 1 1 1 1 1 1   1                          1
```

164.
"The Parsons Beauty". *30EESFT. On dirty brown paper.*

```
6 4 2 4 2 4 2 4 2 4 2 4 2 6 4 2      4 2      4 2      4 2      4 2      4 2      6 4 2 4 2 4 2 4 2 4 2 4 2 6 4 2 4 2 4 2      4 2        6 4 2
                                4 2      4 2      4 2      4 2      4 2      4 2                                              4 2      6 4 2
      3 1      3 1      3 1                                               3 1      3 1      3 1        3 1 3 1 3 1 3 1 5 3 1 5 3 1
5 3 1      3 1      3 1      5 3 1 3 1 3 1 3 1 3 1 3 1 3 1 3 1 3 1 3 1 3 1 3 1 5 3 1      3 1      3 1      5 3 1
```

165.
"Marcy Tefft, her Draft. Orrange Peel." *On the back of an ad for Browns Household Panacea for relieving pain both internal and external, 25 cents a bottle.*

```
1   3                 2   1 3              1 3 5 1 3 5 1 3 5 1   3 2 4 6 2 4 6 2 4 6            2 4   2
2   1   3                  2 4 2 4 6              2 4 6        2           1 3 5           1 3 5 1 3              1   3
    2   1   3              1 3 5 1 3 5                                    2 4 6 2 4 6          1   3   2
        2   1   3          2 4 6 2 4 6        2 4 6        1 3 5        1 3 5 1 3 5         1   3   2
```

166.
"Orange Peel".

```
2 4     1   1   1   1   1   1   1   1   1   1   1   1 3 5 2 4              2 4
1 3 5 2 2 2 2 2 2 2 2 2 2 2 2 2 2 2 2 2 2 2 2 2 2 2 2 4          1 3
    1   1   1   1   1   1   1   1   1   1   1   1          2 4 2 4 2 4
                                                    1 3 1 3      1 3 1 3
```

---

162. Reads either way, standard, condensed #1. Similar to Rose #19, #44, #120 and to Atwater #127 and #130, Cloudless Beauty and Missouri Check.

163. Reads either way, standard and condensed #1. Identical to Rose #245. Similar to Atwater #130, Missouri Check.

164. Right to left, historical, condensed #2. Similar to Rose #191, #192, #195 and #130. A simple Sunflower pattern.

165. Left to right, standard, condensed #2. See also Rose #17, #46, #210 and Atwater #10A, Single Orange Peel.

166. Left to right, standard, condensed #2. Different from Atwater #10A, Orange Peel. See also Rose #30, #31, #32 and Atwater #8, Butternut.

167.
"Peach Sead".

```
      a   a   a   a   a            • •      •     •
  a   a   a   a   a   a            • •            •
  a   a   a       a   a   a         • •   • •           Tramp
a   a   a           a   a          •     • • •    •
```

168.
"Peoneys And Roses In the Wilderness". *On the back of Sun. Suppl. 1896.*

```
 1  1  1  1  1  1  1  11  111  1  11  111  11  3 1
 6 4 6 4 6 4 6 4 6 4 6 4      4    4 4 4      4      4 6 4 2
 1  1  1  1  1  1  1   1       1  1   1      1 1
                   4 6 6  6 6      4 6 6   6 6 4
```

169.
On back of a fish adv. Big Bass.

```
 3 1 3 1   1 3 1 1   3 1 3 1   3 1   3 1   3 1   3 1   3 1   3 1   3 1   3 1 3 1   1 3 1 1   3 1 3 1
 4 2      4 2        4 2 8 4 2 8 4 2 8 4 2 8 4 2 8 4 2 8 4 2 8 4 2 8 4 2 8 4 2      4 2      4 2 4 2
    1        1        1    1    1    1    1    1    1    1        1        3 1
 4 2 8 8  8 8 4 2                                        4 2 8 8  8 8 4 2
```

170.
"P·E·R·R·Y·S V·I·C·T·O·R·Y". *Sept. 10, 1813. On old cardboard. "o" and "r" means red thread.*

```
         o                o    o     o o o    o        o
      1 1          1     1 1 1   1 1 1 1 1   1 1 1    1                          1
 2  2  2     2  2  2  2  2     4 4  6 6   6 6   6 6  4 4     2  2  2  2  2     2  2  2
 1 1 1 1 1 1 1   1 1 1 1 1 1 1 1 1 1 1  1 1    1 1        1 1   1 1 1 1 1 1 1 1 1 1 1 1 1  1 1 1 1 1 1
 2  2  2  2 4 2  2  2  2  2  2 2 4 4  6   6 6  6 6 6  4   4 4 2  2  2  2  2  2 4 2  2  2
```

171.
"Perys Victory". *Much used.*

```
              r     r     r     r     r     r                      r
      1            1     1 1 1   1 1 1 1 1   1 1 1    1                          1
 2  2  2     2  2  2  2  2     6 6  6 6   6 6   6 6  6 6     2  2  2  2  2     2  2  2
 1 1 1 1 1 1   1 1 1 1 1 1 1 1 1 1 1 1  1 1    1 1        1 1   1 1 1 1 1 1 1 1 1 1 1 1  1 1 1 1 1 1
 2  2  2 4 2  2  2  2  2  2  2 4 6   4   6 6  6 6 6  4   6 4 2  2  2  2  2  2 4 2  2  2
```

---

167. Reads either way. This is a strange draft. If threaded literally (as though it were "ones") and treadled as drawn in, it weaves a tiny texture. "Tromp" given is nearly a standard point-twill treadling.

168. Right to left, standard, condensed #3. See Rose #26. A flawed version of Double Chariot Wheels or Church Windows.

169. Right to left, standard, condensed #3. See Rose #26.

170. Reads either way, standard, condensed #2. Almost the same as Atwater #14, Perry's Victory.

171. Reads either way, standard, condensed #2. Virtually identical to Rose #170 except that block sizes differ slightly.

172.

"Pieony lief". *On brown paper. Duplicate in Sun. Sup. 1896.*

```
                                    246246      2424          2424        246246
     13      13      13      13      13      13        13513513      13      13135135
2462424242424242424242424242424246            246        242424        246
135     13      13      13      13      13    135135              1313    1313                135
```

173.

"Pine Burr". *Another pattern uses six threads instead of eight.*

```
135713        13        13        13        13        13                      135713
      24          24        24        24        24        24        2468              2424
          1357      1357      1357      1357      1357      135713571357              13
2468      2468      2468      2468      2468      2468      2468        24682468
```

```
   24          13135713        13          135713        24        1313571357
       2424          2424    24    24        2424    13    2424        2468
13      1313              1313    131313          1313      1313                1357
241324          2468          24    24    242468          24      24        2468        2468
```

174.

"Prim Rose or Prim Rose in Diamonds". *For Mariss Cottrell, 1813.*

```
13      13513513                    13135135
2424246        2424      24    2424      24624
   13          1313513133513          24624
                  1313513133513              13
         246        246    246      246
```

172. Left to right, standard, condensed #2. See also Rose #214, #242; Burnham #258-#264, Monmouth; similar to Atwater #73.

173. Left to right, standard, condensed #2. See also Rose #9 and Atwater #26, Pine Bloom. This draft is a flawed version.

174. Left to right, standard, condensed #2. Almost same as Rose #237. See Atwater #67, World's Wonder.

175.

"Primrose in Diamonds". *1873. Corrected.*

	10		8		6		10		6		8		12	
X X X	4 4 4 4 4	4 4 4 4	4				4 4	4 4 4 4	4 4 4 4					
X X X	3 3 3 3 3			3 3 3			3 3 3			3 3 3 3 3 3				
X X X					2 2	2 2 2 2 2	2						2 2	
X X X		1 1 1 1			1 1 1 1 1			1 1 1 1						

```
    /          Tabby
    /
        3
            2
    6
        3
        3
    7
        3
        3
    6          Use tabby
            7  Repeat
```

176.

"Prusian Diaper #2". *On cardboard back of adv. for brooms. Dated in L.A. scrapbook as "1800 About".*

```
        2 4 6 8          2 4 6 8          2 4 6 8              2 4 6 8          2 4 6 8
    2 4 6 8      2 4 6 8          2 4 6 8          2 4 6 8          2 4 6 8
2 4 6 8              2 4 6 8          2 4 6 8          2 4 6 8          2 4 6 8          2 4 6 8
1 3 5 7 1 3 5 7 1 3 5 7 1 3 5 7 1 3 5 7 1 3 5 7 1 3 5 7 1 3 5 7 1 3 5 7 1 3 5 7 1 3 5 7 1 3 5 7 1 3 5 7 1 3 5 7 1 3 5 7 1 3 5 7
```

```
                          KEY
        2 4 6 8            X X
2 4 6 8                    O O
                           X   X
1 3 5 7 1 3 5 7            O
```

177.

```
    2 4        2 4        2 4            2 4        2 4        2 4
  2 4      2 4          2 4          2 4      2 4          2 4
2 4              2 4        2 4          2 4        2 4        2 4
1 3 1 3 1 3 1 3 1 3 1 3 1 3 1 3 1 3 1 3 1 3 1 3 1 3 1 3 1 3 1 3 1 3 1 3 1 3 1 3 1 3 1 3 1 3
```

175. Reads either way, standard, modern. Woven as drawn in, the pattern is a small Chariot Wheel similar to Atwater #67, World's Wonder.

176. Left to right, condensed #2. Three-block Spot Bronson weave, a "diaper" or concentric diamond pattern. Tie-up given as "key" should be all o's.

177. Left to right, condensed #2. Same as #126 except that spots are 4-thread instead of 8-thread.

178.

"Queenes Fancy".

```
  1  1    1  1  1  1  1  1    1  1      1
   8 8 4 8 8                8 8 4 8 8
 11  1  11  1  1  1  1  1  1  1  11  1  11
 4         4 4 4 4 4 4 4 4 4 4 4 4 4 4        4 4
```

179.

"Rattle Snake". *(Probably recent.)*

```
 2 2 2 2    2 2    6 6 2 6 6        6 6
         2 2    2 2            6 6 2   6
 2   2    2 2    2 6   2  6 6   2 6
    2  2 2    2 2    6   6    6
```

180.

"Rattle Snakes Trail". *On nice square of clean cardboard.*

```
       3 1       3 1 3 1       5 3 1     5 3 1          5 3 1     5 3 1
     4 2 4 2 4 2       4 2 4 2                    6 4 2 6 4 2 4 2 6 4 2 6 4 2
 3 1 3 1     3 1 3 1        3 1 5 3 1      3 1    5 3 1 5 3 1       3 1      5 3 1
 4 2           4 2 4 2      6 4 2 6 4 2 4 2 6 4 2 6 4 2
```

181.

"Red Rose". *On back of one-half adv. for a sale. No date.*

```
 4 2 3 1           4 2 4 2           4 2 4 2 4 2 4 2 4 2 4 2 4 2 4 2 4 2 4 2
   4 2 4 2    4 2 3 1       4 2     4 2     3 1     3 1     3 1     3 1     3 1        3 1    1
     3 1 3 1 3 1      4 2 3 1 4 2 3 1 4 2                                      4 2 4 2 4 2 4 4
 3 1       4 2     3 1 3 1    3 1    3 1 3 1    3 1    3 1     3 1     3 1    3 1 3 1    3 1  1
```

---

178. Reads either way, standard, condensed #1. Different from Atwater #47 Queen's Fancy. A Four Stars & Table pattern similar to Atwater #73 and a simplified Monmouth.

179. Reads either way, historical, stacked. Error: in final (right) column, the lower 6 should be moved down 1 row to the second row. This pattern is similar to Atwater #39, Rattlesnake or Wandering Vine.

180. Right to left, standard, condensed #2. A variant of Rose #179; looks like diagonal short-stem roses.

181. Right to left, standard, condensed #3. The Cross Compass.

182.
"Rockey Mt. Cucumber".

```
2 4 6          2 4 6 2 4 6 2 4 6        2 4 6 2 4 6      1 3 5      2 4 6 2 4 6 2 4 6      1 3 5      2 4 6 2 4 6 2 4 6
       1 3 5 1 3 5      1 3 5 1 3 5        1 3 5          1 3 5      1 3 5          1 3 5      1 3 5
    2 4 6 2 4 6          2 4 6 2 4 6      1 3 5      1 3 5          1 3 5      1 3 5              1 3 5
1 3 5 1 3 5          1 3 5      1 3 5 1 3 5      2 4 6 2 4 6 2 4 6      1 3 5      2 4 6 2 4 6 2 4 6      1 3 5      2 4 6
```

```
1 3 5      2 4 6 1 3 5 1 3 5      1 3 5          1 3 5 1 3 5 1 3 5          1 3 5 1 3 5      1 3      1 3      1 3      1 3      1 3
       1 3 5      2 4 6          2 4 6 2 4 6      2 4 6 2 4 6          2 4 6 2 4 6 2 4 2 4 2 4 2 4 2 4 2 4 2 4 2 4
    1 3 5          1 3 5      1 3 5 1 3 5          1 3 5 1 3 5      1 3 5      1 3      1 3      1 3      1 3
2 4 6 2 4 6      2 4 6      2 4 6 2 4 6 2 4 6      2 4 6      2 4 6 2 4 6
```

```
    1 3      1 3      1 3      1 3      1 3      1 3      1 3      1 3      1 3      1 3      1 3      1 3      1 3 5
2 4 2 4 2 4 2 4 2 4 2 4 2 4 2 4 2 4 2 4 2 4 2 4 2 4 2 4 2 4 2 4 2 4 2 4 2 4 2 4 2 4 2 4 2 4 2 4 2 4 2 4 2 4 6 2 4 6
1 3      1 3      1 3      1 3      1 3      1 3      1 3      1 3      1 3      1 3      1 3      1 3 5
```

183.

```
2 4 6          2 4 6 2 2 4 6          2 4 6 2      2 4 6      2 1 3 5 1 3      2 4 6      2 1 3 5
       1 3 5      1 3 5 1 3 5      1 3          1 3      2      2 4 6      1 3
    2 4 6 2 4 6          2 4 6 2 4 6      1 3      2          1 3      2
1 3 5 1 3 5          1 3      1 3 5 1 3 5      2 1 3 5 1 3      2 4 6      2 1 3 5 1 3      2 4 6
```

```
2          2 4 6      1 3 2 4 6 2      2 4 6 2 1 3 5      1 3 5 1 3 2 4 6          2 4 6 2 4 6
1 3          2      1 3          1 3      2 4 6 2 4 6      1 3 5 1 3 5          1 3 5 1 3 5
    1 3      2          1 3          1 3 5 1 3 5      2 4 6 2 4 6          2 4 6
    2 1 3 5 1 3      1 3 5      2 1 3 5      2 4 6 2 4 6          2      1 3 5 1 3 5
```

```
2   2   2   2   2   2   2   2   2   2   2   2   2   2      2 4 6 2
1 1 1 1 1 1 1 1 1 1 1 1 1 1 1 1 1 1 1 1 1 1 1 1 1 1 1 1 1 1 1 1 1 1 1 1 1 1 1 1 1 3 5 1 3 5 1 1
2   2   2   2   2   2   2   2   2   2   2   2   2   2   2 2 4 6      2
```

182. Left to right, standard, condensed #2.
183. Left to right, standard, condensed #2. Note that the third line is on upper 3 rows.

184.
"Rose and Diamond".

			1 1				1 1			1 1					1 1
	1 1			1 1			1 1				1 1		1 1
1 1		1 1			1 1					1 1
					1 1
1 1 1 1 1 1 1 1 1 1 1 1 1 1 1 1 1 1 1 1 1 1 1 1 1 1 1 1 1

	1 1
		1 1
			1 1
1 1
1 1 1 1 1 1 1 1

Tread.

A	B	C	D	E
5	2	5	5	2
2	5	2	3	5
5	1	5	5	2
3	5	2	3	5
5	1	5	5	1
3	5	3	4	5
5	2	5	5	1
4	5	3	4	5
5	2	5	5	
4	5	4	3	
5	3	5	5	
3	5	4	3	
5	3	5	5	
3	5	2		
5	4	5		
2	5	2		
5	2			

Tie frames 4-5 to treadle 1.
Tie frames 3-3 to treadle 2.
Tie frames 2-5 to treadle 3.
Tie frames 1-3-5 to treadle 4.
Tie frames 1-2-3-4 to treadle 5.

Treadles 1-5 are plain weave. 2-3-4 are rose. Two threads to a split.

185.
"Rose and Diamonds. Barley Corn." *Not complete.*

2 2		2 2		2 2		2	2 2			2 2
	2 2	2 2		2 2		2		2 2	2 2
		2 2		2 2		2 2			2 2
2 2						2 2
1 1 1 1 1 1 1 1 1 1 1 1 1 1 1 1 1 1 1 1 1 1 1 1 1 1 1 1 1 1 1 1 1 1 1 1

186.
"Double Roses". *A.D. 1700 Va.,*
on piece of box. Very pretty — distinct.

1		1		1 1		1		1
	1 1 1	1 1 1	1	1 1 1	1 1 1	1
4		4			4		4
6 6	4 4 4	6 6 2 6 6	4 4 4	6 6 2

---

184. Right to left, ones. A four-block Spot Bronson weave. Note that in the tie-up, a "5" is bottom row and "1" is top row of threading. Tie-up and treadling given have flaws, but a standard tie-up and as drawn in treadling weaves a pattern which in block form resembles Rose #180, the "shortstem rosebuds".

185. Reads either way, condensed #2. Four-block spot Bronson. Pattern is a flawed version of #184.

186. Reads either way, historical, condensed #2. Same as Rose #8. Similar to Atwater #30A Sweet Briar Beauty.

187.
"Rose in the Blossom". *On Sun. Sup. 1896. Pasted on cardboard. Dirty.*

```
1 2    1 5 4    1 1 1 5    4 4    1 1 5      1 5      1 1 5        4 6 4
   1 5 4 2 1 1 1              1 1        2 1                    1 1 1 1 1 1
        1    4 4 6 1 1      6 4    2        4 2      2 1      2 4 4 4
6            1 6 4 4 4 2 1    1 1  5 4      1 7 2 1 5 4 4  2 1 5
```

188.

```
1 3 5 7 9  2 4    1 3 5 7    2 4        1 7    1 3    1 7      2 4 2 4    1 3 1 3        1 7      1 3
           1 3 5 2 4 2 4 6  1 3 1 3 1 3                  1 3            2 4 2 4
                 1 3        2 4    2 4  2        1 3    1 3    8 2 4        2 4      1 3  2      2 4 5
2 4 6 8 10                        1   9    2    2 4 2 4 2 4    2  1    1 3 1 3 1 3 2 4      1  9 2 6 1 3 5 2 4
```

```
   1 7      2 4    2 6    2 4
        1 3 1 3 1 3 1 5 1 3 1 3
1 3      8 2 4    2 4    2 4
2 4    2 1
```

189.
"ROSE IN THE WILDERNESS". *On wrapping paper.*

```
      4 2 4 2        4 2 4 2        4 2 4 2        4 2 4 2        4 2 4 2        4 2 4 2      4 2 4 2
4 2 4 2        4 2 4 2        4 2 4 2        4 2 4 2        4 2 4 2        4 2 4 2        4 2        4 2
3 1        3 1 3 1        3 1 3 1        3 1 3 1        3 1 3 1        3 1 3 1        3 1        3 1 3 1
   3 1 3 1        3 1 3 1        3 1 3 1        3 1 3 1        3 1 3 1        3 1 3 1      3 1 3 1
```

```
4 2      4 2    6 4 2 4 2 4 2 4 2 4 2 4 2 4 2 4 2 4 2 4 2 4 2 4 2 4 2 4 2 4 2 4 2 6 4 2      4 2      4 2      6 4 2
   4 2      4 2                                                                          4 2      4 2      4 2
            3 1    3 1    3 1    3 1    3 1    3 1    3 1    3 1
3 1 3 1 3 1 3 1 1        3 1    3 1    3 1    3 1    3 1    3 1    3 1    5 3 1 3 1 3 1 3 1 3 1 3 1 5 3 1
```

```
6 4 2    4 2    4 2
   4 2    4 2    4 2
5 3 1 3 1 3 1 3 1 3 1 3 1
```

---

187. Left to right, standard, condensed #2. Variant of The Cross Compass.

188. Left to right, standard, condensed #3. Flawed version of #187.

189. Right to left, historical, condensed #3. Different than Atwater #20, Rose in the Wilderness. This is a radiating and sunflower combination.

190.
"Rose Leaf and Bud".

```
1    2 3    4 4    2 1    1    1 2    4 4    3 2    1 3 3 3 3 3 3 3 3 3 3 3 3 3
  1 1    4 4    4 4    1 1    1 1    3 4    4 4    1 1
1 1    3 4    4 4    1 1        1 1    4 4    4 3    1 1    3 3 3 3 3 3 3
  1 2    4 4    4 2    1 1 1    2 3    4 4    2 1    3 3 3 3 3 3 3
```

191.
"R·O·S·E O·F T·H·E V·A·L·L·E·Y". "RoSE oF THE VALEY". *Sun. Sup. 1896.*

```
      2 4 6 4 4 4 2 4 6        4   4   4              4   4   4
    1 3 5 1 3 5   1   1 3 5 1 3 5        1 1 1 1 1 1
2 4 6 2 4 6              2 4 6 2 4 6   6   6   2 4 6 4 4 4 4 4 4 4 4 4 4 4 2 4 6   4   4
1 3 5        1   1        1 3 5 1 1 1 1 1 1 3 5   1   1   1   1   1   1 3 5 1 1 1 1 1
```

192.
On Sunday Supplement 1896.

```
      2 4 2 4 2 4 2 4 2 4        2 4    2 4    2 4                                   2 4    2 4    2 4
    1 3 1 3    1 3    1 3 1 3              1 3    1 3    1 3    1 3    1 3    1 3    1 3
2 4 2 4              2 4 2 4    2 4    2 4    2 4 2 4 2 4 2 4 2 4 2 4 2 4 2 4 2 4 2 4 2 4 2 4 2 4    2 4    2 4
1 3        1 3    1 3        1 3 1 3 1 3 1 3 1 3 1 3 1 3    1 3    1 3    1 3    1 3    1 3    1 3    1 3 1 3 1 3 1 3 1 3 1 3
```

193.
"ROSE of the Valley". *Sunday Sup. 1896.*

```
2 4    2 4    2 4    2 4        2 4    2 4    2 4        2 4 2 4    2 4 2 4        2 4    2 4    2 4
1 3 1 3 1 3 1 3 1 3 1 3 1 3 1 3                      1 3 1 3          1 3 1 3
  2 4    2 4    2 4    2 4 2 4    2 4    2 4    2 4 2 4        2 4        2 4 2 4    2 4    2 4
          1 3 1 3 1 3 1 3 1 3 1 3 1 3        1 3 1 3 1 3        1 3 1 3 1 3 1 3 1 3 1 3
```

```
    2 4    2 4    2 4
  1 3 1 3 1 3 1 3 1 3 1 3 1 3
2 4 2 4    2 4    2 4    2 4
1 3
```
3 × 24 ends on each side for the border. 480 ends for tidy.

---

190. Reads either way, historical, stacked. A simplified version of Atwater #115, Double Bow Knot (and several other names).

191. Left to right, standard, condensed #3. Almost identical to #192 and #193. A single Sunflower.

192. Left to right, standard, condensed #2. Almost identical to #191 and #193.

193. Left to right, standard, condensed #2. See also Rose #130 and #163. A variant of The Cross Compass.

194.
"Red Rose".

```
  4   4        4   4         4   4         4   4           4   4        4   4        4   4
3 3 3 3 3 3 3 3 3 3 3 3 3 3 3 3 3
    2   2        2   2         2   2         2 2 2 2       2   2         2   2
                                        1 1 1 1 1 1 1 1 1 1 1 1 1 1
```

```
       4   4   4   4        4   4   4   4         4   4         4   4         4   4
    3   3   3   3        3   3   3   3                                            3   3
2   2   2   2           2   2        2 2 2 2       2   2         2   2       2   2   2   2
1 1 1           1 1 1 1 1         1 1 1 1 1 1 1 1 1 1 1 1 1 1 1 1 1
```

195.
"True Loves Rest". *On Sun. Sup. 1896.*

```
      2 4 6 2 4 2 4 2 4 2 4 6          2 4      2 4      2 4
   1 3 5 1 3 5     1 3     1 3 5 1 3 5            1 3     1 3     1 3     1 3     1 3
2 4 6 8 2 4 6                  2 4 6 2 4 6   2 4      2 4      2 4 6 2 4 2 4 2 4 2 4 2 4 2 4 2 4 2 4 2 4 2 4
1 3 5 7        1 3     1 3             1 3 5 1 3 1 3 1 3 1 3 1 3 1 3 5    1 3     1 3     1 3     1 3
```

```
       2 4      2 4      2 4
   1 3
2 4 2 4 2 4 6     2 4      2 4
1 3    1 3 5 1 3 1 3 1 3 1 3 1 3
```

196.
"The Royal Beauty. A coverlet." *Old pattern on wood; no date.*

```
1  7  2          2  1  3          2  1  5          2  1  7   2 2 2 2 2 2 2 2 2 2 2 2 2 2 2 2 2 2   8    2 4
      1        2  1  3        2  1  5        2  1  7   1 3 1 1 1 1 1 1 1 1 1 1 1 1 1 3   1 3
   2     2  1  3        2  1  5        2  1  7   2 4                              2 4  2 4
2  1  1  3        2  1  5        2  1  7        2       1 1 1 1 1 1 1 1 1 1   1    1 3
```

```
   2       1 3    1    2 2 2 2 2 2 2 2 2 2 2 2 2 2 2 2 2 2
1 3       2 4    2 4    2  1 1 1 1 1 1 1 1 1 1 1
2 4    1 3    1 3    1  3
   1  7   2 4    8    1 1 1 1 1 1 1 1 1
```

```
   1 1  7          2  1  5          2  1  3            1
1  5    2  1  7          2  1  5          2  1  3    2
2           2  1  7          2  1  5          2  1 3 1
   8           2  1  5          2  1  3          2 4  2
```

194. Reads either way, standard, modern. Same as #193 with smaller table.

195. Left to right, standard, condensed #2. Same as #191 and #194.

196. Left to right, standard, condensed #3. Same as Rose #134. Related to Atwater #106, Sunrise on the Walls of Troy.

197.
"Saint Ann's Robe. N.C." *(See #220.)*

```
1 1 1 1 1 1 1 1 1 1 1 1 1 1 1 1 1 1 1 1 1 1 1 1 1   4 4   4 4   2     2 2     2 2     2 2     2   4 4   4 4   1 1 1 1
                                            4 4   2   4 4   2 4 2   4   2 4 2   4   2 4 2   4   2 4 2   4 4   2   4 4
 1 1 1 1 1 1 1 1 1 1 1 1 1   4 4   4 4   2 2     2 2     2 2     2 2   4 4     4 4   1 1
 1 1 1 1 1 1 1 1 1 1 1 1 1 6   4 2 4   4 2   4   2 4 2   4   2 4 2   4   2 4 2   4   2 4   4 2 4   4 1 1
```

198.
"Salleys Fancy". *Sun. sup. 1896.*

```
6 2 4 6         6 2 4   2 4 6         6 2 4   2 4 6         6 2 4   2 4 6         6 2 4
    1 2 4 6 2 4   6       2 4 6 2 4   6       2 4 6 2 4   6       2 4 6 2 4
    1 3   1 3 1         1 1 3   1 3 1         1 1 3   1 3 1         1 1 3   1 3 1
1 1 3       1         1 3 1 1 3       1         1 3 1 1 3       1         1 3 1 1 3       1         1 3
```

199.
"SARAH LIS PATTERN".

```
                  1 1   1 3   1         1   3 2 4   2             1 1   1 3   1 1
 1 1 1 1 1   1 3   6 6       6 6   1   3   2       1   3   2         6 6       6 6
 2 2 2 2 2 2 2 2 2 2 2 4 2 4   1 1 2 4 1 1   1   3   2             1   3   2     1 1       1 1
 1 1 1 1 1 1 3   6     6     6     2         1 3       1   3 6   6 2 4 6       6
```

```
 2 4     1   1   1   1   1   1   1
 1 3 2 4 2 2 2 2 2 2 2 2 2 2 2 2 2 2
    1 3   1   1   1   1   1   1
```

---

197. Reads either way, historical, stacked.

198. Left to right, historical, condensed #3. In the first (left) and fourth columns, the 1's should each be on the second row, not the lowest or third. Similar to Atwater #1, Russian Diaper (with a small star inserted).

199. Left to right, standard, condensed #3. Error: in 19th and 20th columns from left, the 2 and 4 should be on the lowest row. The pattern is related to Burnham #332-#333, Indian Plains.

200.

"The 7 Stars", "The Isle of Patmos", "Sea Star", "See Shell". *This is all one pattern; different names in different states.*

```
      4  4  4  4  4  4  4  4                                          4   4
   3  3              3  3  3  3  3  3  3  3              3  3           3  3  3  3
   2  2                    2  2  2  2  2  2  2  2  2  2  2  2  2  2  2
      1  1  1  1                 1  1  1  1        1  1  1  1
```

```
   4  4        4  4  4  4                                   4  4  4  4
         3  3        3  3  3  3           3  3        3  3  3  3        3  3
            2  2           2  2  2  2  2  2  2  2  2  2  2  2  2  2  2        2  2
   1  1        1  1              1  1  1  1        1  1  1  1        1  1
```

```
   4  4  4  4                                4  4  4  4        4  4  4  4
         3  3  3  3              3  3        3  3  3  3     3  3        3  3
               2  2  2  2  2  2  2  2  2  2  2  2  2  2  2        2  2
   1  1              1  1  1  1        1  1  1  1        1  1        1  1
```

```
                                             4  4  4  4  4  4  4  4        4  4
   3  3              3  3              3  3  3  3  3  3  3  3        3  3
   2  2  2  2  2  2  2  2  2  2  2  2  2  2  2  2  2                 2  2
         1  1  1  1        1  1  1  1                    1  1  1  1        1  1
```

```
   4           4  4  4        4  4  4        4  4  4        4  4  4        4  4  4
         3  3        3  3           3  3           3  3           3  3           3  3
      2  2        2  2        2  2        2  2        2  2        2  2
   1        1  1  1        1  1  1        1  1  1        1  1  1        1  1  1
```

```
   4  4  4           4  4  4        4  4  4
         3  3              3  3
            2  2           2  2
   1  1  1        1  1  1        1  1  1
```

200. Left to right, standard, modern. This pattern is different from the one Atwater calls Seven Stars (#47). It is the same as Atwater #27, Gentleman's Fancy, which is similar to Pine Bloom designs. See also Rose #202, #203 and #218.

201.
"Shuckeroon's Fancy". *On rather mussed brown paper.*

```
    3 1      3 1      3 1           5 3 1 3 1      3 1 3 1 3 1            4 2          4 2 4 2 4 2      4 2
                6 4 2 6 4 2       4 2 4 2      4 2 4 2            3 1 3 1      3 1 3 1 3 1
5 3 1      3 1      3 1      5 3 1 5 3 1         3 1 3 1          3 1 3 1      4 2 4 2              4 2
6 4 2 4 2 4 2 4 2 4 2 4 2 6 4 2         4 2 4 2       4 2        4 2 5 3 1 3 1        3 1
```

```
    3 1          3 1 3 1 1      1 3 1          3 1 1         1 3 1 3 1          3 1      3 1 3 1 5 3 1
        4 2 4 2      2 6 4 2 2      6 4 2      2 6 4 2 2      4 2 4 2            4 2 4 2      6 4 2 6 4 2
3 1      3 1 3 1          5 3 1      1 5 3 1 1      5 3 1          3 1 3 1      3 1 3 1            5 3 1
4 2 4 2 4 2         4 2          4 2 2      2 4 2          4 2      4 2 4 2 4 2      4 2
```

```
    4 2 4 2         5 3 1      3 1 3 1 3 1         3 1 5 3 1           3 1      3 1      3 1          5 3 1 3 1 3 1
3 1 3 1      3 1          4 2 4 2      4 2 4 2          6 4 2 6 4 2                  6 4 2 6 4 2      4 2 4 2
4 2          4 2 4 2      3 1 3 1          3 1 3 1          5 3 1 5 3 1      3 1      3 1      5 3 1 5 3 1            3 1
      3 1      3 1 6 4 2 4 2          4 2      4 2 4 2          6 4 2 4 2 4 2 4 2 4 2 4 2 4 2 6 4 2            4 2
```

202.
"7 Stars". *Back of adv. for Pilgrim Baking powder; quite torn and fly specked.*

```
    1 1           1 3 1 3      2 4 2 4                2 4 2 4      2 4 2 4              2 4 2 4      1 3
2 4    8 8    2 4    2 4 2 4      1 3      1 3 1 3    1 3    1 3 1 3      1 3      1 3 1 3    1 3    1 3 1 3      2 4
1 3    1 1 1 3 1 1 3         2 4         2 4 8 2 4 8 2 4         2 4         2 4 8 2 4 8 2 4         1 3
    8    8    8         2 4    1 3         1    1         1 3    1 3         1    1         1 3    2 4
```

```
1 3            8 8    1 3 5      2 4 6      2 4 6      2 4 6      2 4 6      2 4 6      2 4 6      2 4 6      2 4 6      2 4 6
2 4 2 4    1 3    1 1    1 3         1 3         1 3         1 3         1 3         1 3         1 3         1 3         1 3
    1 3 8 2 4 8 8         2 4         2 4         2 4         2 4         2 4         2 4         2 4         2 4
        1    1    1      2 4 6      1 3 5      1 3 5      1 3 5      1 3 5      1 3 5      1 3 5      1 3 5      1 3 5
```

203.
"Seven Stars from N. Carolina: 'Handsome'."

```
 10          10    10      2    2         10    10      2    2         10    10      2    2         10    10         10    6    6    6    6    6    6    6    6    6
2    10 10      2    2 2    2 2      2    2 2    2 2      2    2 2    2 2      2    10 10      2    2    2    2    2    2    2    2    2
2          10 10 2 10 2         2      2 10 2 10 2         2      2 10 2 10 2         2      2 10 2 10 10         2    2    2    2    2    2    2    2    2
    10 10            2 2    2 2         2 2    2 2         2 2    2 2         10 10      6    6    6    6    6    6    6    6    6
```

201. Right to left, standard, condensed #2. A flawed compound pattern of blooming left and partial wheels.

202. Left to right, standard, condensed #3. Different from Atwater Seven Stars. Same as Rose #200, #203 and #218, and Atwater #27, Gentleman's Fancy.

203. Reads either way, historical, stacked. Same as #202 on larger scale; see also Rose #200, #218.

204.
"Sister Blankets. Coverlet. 2 Harness."

```
1 1 1 1 1 1 1 1 1 6 6 6 6 6 6 6 6 6 6 1 1 1 1 1 1 1 1 1 6 6 6 1 1 1 6 6 6 1 1 1 6 6 6 1 1 1 6 6 6 1 1 1 6 6 6
6 6 6 6 6 6 6 6 6 1 1 1 1 1 1 1 1 1 6 6 6 6 6 6 6 6 6 1 1 1 6 6 6 1 1 1 6 6 6 1 1 1 6 6 6 1 1 1 6 6 6 1 1 1
```

205.
"Snails Trail".

1 3 1 3		1 3 1 3		1 3 1 3		1 3 5 1 3 5 1 1 1		1	
	2 4 2 4		2 4 2 4		2 4 2 4		2 4 6 6	6 6 2 4 6	
	1 3 1 3		1 3 1 3		1 3 1 3		1 1 1	1 3 5
2 4		2 4 2 4		2 4 2 4		2 4 2 4 6	2 6 6 2	

206.
"Double Snowball and Compass". *1700 VA. "Composed of Diamonds, Squares, Circles & Ovals".* Mrs. Beals.

1 1	1	1 1	1	1 1	1	1	1	1 1	1	1 1	1	1 1			
	1 1	1 1	1	1	10 1	1	1	1 10	1	1	1 1	1 1	1	END
4 4		4 4		4 4 10 4 10 4 4			4 4		4 4		
4	4 4 4	8 8 2 8 8			8 8 2 8 8	4 4 4		4 4		

---

204. Reads either way, condensed #1. Two-shaft (usually weft-faced on opposites, no tabby). Block design is similar to Atwater #153 and #161, a nameless pattern and Lasting Beauty.

205. Left to right, standard, condensed #3. Same as Rose #137. Similar to Atwater #38, an imperfect Cat Tracks.

206. Reads either way, historical, condensed #2. Errors: in 14th and 22nd columns from left, the 10's on the third row should be moved down to the second row. See also Rose #158 and #220. This pattern is the same as Atwater #79, Lover's Knot (which is Whig Rose when treadled rose-fashion).

207.
"Snow Balls". *Sun. Sup. 1896.*

```
            2 4 2 4              2 4 2 4 2 4                      2 4 2 4 2 4 2 4 2 4 2 4 2 4 2 4
   1 3      1 3      1 3            1 3      1 3         1 3         1 3     1 3      1 3     1 3      1 3     1 3    1 3    1 3
2 4 2 4 2 4 2 4 2 4        2 4 2 4 2 4 2 4 2 4        2 4 2 4 2 4 2 4 2 4
1 3      1 3      1 3      1 3 1 3      1 3      1 3 1 3      1 3 1 3      1 3      1 3 1 3      1 3      1 3     1 3
```

```
2 4 2 4 2 4 2 4 2 4 2 4 2 4 2 4 2 4 2 4
   1 3      1 3      1 3      1 3      1 3
```

```
1 3      1 3      1 3      1 3      1 3      1 3
```

208.

```
1 1 1 1 1  2              2 4          1   3 1 1 1 1 1  2               2 4          1   3
  8   8   1   3   2               1   3   2   8   8   1   3   2                 1   3   2
              1   3   2        1   3   2                   1   3   2       1   3   2
8   4   8            1   3 1 3   2           8   4   8        1   3 1 3   2
```

```
1 1 1 1 1  2                                                                              1   3
  8   8   1   3   2         1 3 5  4  4  4  4  4  4  4  4  4  4  4  4  2 4         1   3   2
              1   3   2         1 1 1 1 1 1 1 1 1 1 1 1 1 1 1 1 1 1 1 1 1 1 1 1    1   3   2
8   4   8            1   3 2 4  8  8  8  8  8  8  8  8  8  8  8  8 1 3 5   2
```

209.

```
      2 4 2 4 2 4            2 4 2 4 2 4           2 4 2 4 2 4 2 4
  2 4    2 4      1 3        2 4    2 4      1 3      2 4    2 4      1 3      1 3
2 1 3 2 1 3 2             2 1 3 2 1 3 2           2 1 3 2 1 3 2
1      1     1 1 3      1 3 1      1      1 1 3      1 3 1      1     1 1 3      1 3      1 3
```

210.
"Squares and Diamonds".

```
3 3     2 2  2 2     3 3
  3 2     2   2     2 3     4   4   4
    2 2     2     2 2     4 4 4 4 4 4 4
3     2 2   2   2 2     3 4   4   4   4
```

207. Left to right, standard, condensed #2. See Atwater #57. A flawed, simplified Nine Snowballs.

208. Left to right, standard, condensed #3. In second line, 15th to 17th columns from left, the 1, 3, 5 should be moved up one row to the top row. There are many breaks in the tabby order in this draft because of inverted blocks. This pattern is different from Atwater's Snowballs. It is the same as Rose #219, #224 and #225 and Atwater #56, Granite State.

209. Left to right, standard, condensed #2. This draft has many and frequent breaks in tabby order because of inverted blocks. It is a flawed Dog Track variant, different from the one Atwater calls Snowballs.

210. Reads either way, standard, stacked. See also Rose #17, #46, #165 and #210. Similar to Atwater #10A, Orange Peel.

211.
"Sun Flower". *1700 Va A.D. A beauty on brown paper.*

```
1    1 1 1     1   1   1   1   1   1   1   1   1   1      1 1 1      1
  1 1        1 1  1   1   1   1   1   1   1   1   1 1       1 1   1
  6   2   2   6 6 2 6 2 6 2 6 2 6 2 6 2 6 2 6 2 6 6      2   2   6   6
s4  6   6   6                                      6   6   6   4
```

Tread.

2-3	2-3
1-4	1-4
1-3	1-3
2-3	2-3
1-3	1-3
1-4	1-4
2-4	2-4
1-4	1-4
2-3	2-3
1-3	1-3
2-3	2-3
2-4	2-4
2-3	2-3
2-4	2-4
2-3	2-3
2-4	2-4
2-3	2-3
2-4	
center	

212.
"Summer and Winter". *A handsome Draft, Abigal Stedman, 1821. On brown paper.*

```
1 1 1 1 1   1   1 1   1 3   1 1   1 3   1 1 1 1 1 1 1 1
8   8   8          8   2 4  8          8   8   8   8
      1   1    1     1     1     1
  2   2   6 6 4 6 6   6    6   6 6 2 4 6 6   2   2   2   2
```

213.

```
1          1          1          1          1        2   3 7   2
2   2    1   3 2   2    1   3 4   2    1   3 2   2    1   3 2   2    2 6            1
1   3 2   2    1   3 2   2    1   3 2   2    1   3    2    1   3 2    1 5      1   3 2
    1          1          1          1          1 1   3   4 1   3   2
```

```
  1   3   4 1   3      1          1          1          1
      1 5      1   3 2 2    1   3 2 2      1   3 2   2    1   3 2 2      1   3
2       2 6    2   2    1   2    2    1   2   2 2    1   3 2   2    1   2   2
1   3   2   3 7   2   1      1   3        1   3 1          1          1   3
```

214.

```
2 4 2 4       2 4        6 2 4 6 2 4 6 2 4 6 2 4 6 2 4 6 2 4 6 2 4 6 2 4 6      2 4        2 4
  1 3 1 3       1 3 1  1   1   1   1   1   1   1   1   1 1 3       1 3 1 3
    2 4 2 4    2 4 2 4                                         2 4 2 4    2 4 2 4
1 3        1 3 1 3 1 3    1 3   1 3   1 3   1 3   1 3   1 3   1 3   1 3   1 3    1 3 1 3 1 3
```

---

211. Reads either way, historical, condensed #2. Pattern is different from the type Atwater calls Sunflower. It is similar to Rose #12 and is a variant of Atwater #82, The Arrow. Treadling given is twill-like with a table.

212. Left to right, standard, condensed #3. Summer & winter is the pattern name, not the weave (which is overshot). Same as Rose #216, Troy's Beauty, and Atwater #49, The Eliza Ray coverlet.

213. Left to right, standard, condensed #3. Overshot, a flawed version of Rose #47. See also Rose #160 and #239.

214. Left to right, standard, condensed #3. Overshot. See also Rose #172, #242, Atwater #73 and Burnham #258-#264, Monmouth.

215.

"From Coverlet woven by Abigail Stedman about 1815. Drawn for Mr. W.H.H. Rose by his grateful friend Laura M. Allen. (Mrs. Will H. Allen). Aug. 30, 1912.

```
5 3 1          1  1  7 5 3 1 1                                              5 3 1   2   2
       5 3 1   2 2 2 8 6 4 2      3 1    3 1    3 1    3 1    3 1      4 2   5 3 1 3  3
     4 2 6 4 2 2 1  1        4 2 4 2 4 2 4 2 4 2 4 2 4 2 4 2 4 2 4 2 5 3 1 5 3 1      4   4
6 4 2 5 3 1              2 5 3 1    3 1    3 1    3 1    3 1    3 1    6 4 2 6 4 2  1  1
```

```
       7 5 3 1  4 2 5 3 1 3 1 3 1 1 5 3 1 5 3 1
8 6 4 2          5 3 1       4 2   2       6 4 2
7 5 3 1 3 1
       4 2 8 6 4 2         4 2    4 2  6 4 2
```

Tread by draft.
Plain weave 1-3 2-4.

216.

"Troys Beauty. 1826." *On small piece of brown paper.*

```
1 1 1 1 1  1  1 1  1  1 1  1  1 1 1 1 1 1 1 1 1
10   10   10        10  4  10        10   10   10   10
            1  1    1  1    1  1
2   2   6 6 4 6 6   6  6   6 6 4 6 6   2   2   2   2
```

217.

"The Blooming Leaf".

```
                   1 1   3 3   6 6 6 6   2 2   2 2       2 2   2 2   6 6 6 6   3 3      1
3  3  3  3  3  3  3  3   1 2   3 2   6  66   2 2    2 1  2 2   2 2   6 6  6    2 3    2 1
3 3 3 3 3 3 3 3 3 3 3 3 3 3 3 3   2 2   2 2      6 2   2 2    1 6 2   2 2   2 6      2 2   2 2
3  3  3  3  3  3  3  3 1   2 3   2 6  6   2 2    2 2   6   2 2    2 2   6  6 2    3 2
```

218.

"Seven Stars".

```
10 10         2 2  2 2        2 2  2 2         2 2  2 2         10 10  6  6  6  6  6  6  6  6  6
2    10 10  2    2 2  2  2 2   2   2 2  2  2 2   2   2 2  2  2 10 2   10 10  2  2  2  2  2  2  2  2  2
2    10 10 2 10 2   2    2 10 2 10 2   2   2 10 2 10 2   2   2 10 2 10 10    2  2  2  2  2  2  2  2  2
10       10   10   2  2    10   10   2  2    10   10   2  2    10   10    10  6  6  6  6  6  6  6  6
```

215. Right to left, standard, condensed #2. Identical to Rose #133. An uncorrected Velvet Rose type; see also Atwater #145, The Warner Coverlet.

216. Reads either way, standard, condensed #2. Same as Rose #212. See also Atwater #49, The Eliza Ray coverlet.

217. Reads either way, standard, stacked. See also Rose #18 and Atwater #112, Blooming Leaf.

218. Reads either way, standard, stacked. Both 10's in the 26th column should be moved down 1 row to the lowest 2 rows.

219.
"The Snow Balls".

```
1 1 1 1 1   2                   2 4           1   3 1 1 1 1 1   2                   2 4           1   3 1 1 1 1 1
    8   8   1   3   2                   1   3   2   8   8   1   3   2                   1   3   2   8   8       2
            1   3   2       1   3   2                           1   3   2       1   3   2                   1   3   2
8   4   8           1   3 1 3   2               8   4   8           1   3 1 3   2               8   4   8       1   3
```

```
1 3 5   4     4     4     4     4     4     4     4     4     4       4   4
      1 1 1 1 1 1 1 1 1 1 1 1 1 1 1 1 1 1 1 1 1 1 1 1 1 1 1 1 1 1 1
2 4 8   8     8     8     8     8     8     8     8     8     8       8   8
```

220.
"Cumpass Work".

```
1 3 1 3         1 3 1 3 1 3         2 4 2 4                     2 4 6 8 2 4 2 4 6 8 2 4 2 4 6 8 2 4 2 4 6 8
2 4         2 4 2 4     2 4 2 4         1 3 1 3     1 3     1 3 1 3 5 7     1 3 5 7     1 3 5 7     1 3 5 7 1 3
    1 3 1 3             1 3 1 3         2 4 2 4 2 4 2 4 2 4                                                 2 4
    2 4 2 4         2 4         2 4 1 3         1 3     1 3             1 3         1 3         1 3
```

```
        2 4 2 4         2 4 2 4 2 4         2 4 2 4
    1 3     1 3 1 3         1 3 1 3     1 3 1 3         1 3
2 4 2 4 2 4 2 4         2 4 2 4         2 4 2 4
1 3     1 3         1 3 1 3         1 3         1 3 1 3
```

221.
"Jay's Fancy".

```
    4     4   4   8   8       4       8   8   4
                  1   1   1           1 1 1 1 1
4     4     4   8   4   8 4   4 8   4   8
1 1 1 1 1       1       1 1 1 1                   1
```

222.
"Guess Me — N.C."

```
1 1 1 1 1 1 1 1 1 1 1 1 1 1 1 1 1 1 1 1 1 1   4 4     4 4     2       2 2       2 2       2 2       2
                                            4 4   2     4 4   2 4 2       2 4 2       2 4 2       2 4 2 4 4
1   1   1   1   1   1   1   1   1   1   1   4 4       4 4     2 2       2 2       2 2       2 2       4
  1   1   1   1   1   1   1   1   1   1   1 4     4 2 4       4 2   4   2 4 2   4   2 4 2   4   2 4 2   4   2 4
```

"Saint Ann's Robe — N.C."

```
4 4     4 4       1 1 1 1 1 1 1
    2       4 4
4         4 4     1   1   1
  4 2 4       4 1   1   1   1
```

219. Left to right, standard, condensed #3. In Columns 34-36 from left edge, the 1, 3 and 5 should be moved up one row to the top row. There are several flaws in this draft. It is different from Atwater's Snowballs, but is the same as Rose #208, #224, #225 and Atwater #56, Granite State.

220. Left to right, standard, condensed #2. See also Rose #206 and Atwater #79, a Lover's Knot variant.

221. Reads either way, standard, condensed #2. Pattern is same as Rose #94, a flawed variant of 4-Leaved Clover on Opposites, Atwater #64.

222. Reads either way, historical, stacked. Both names (Guess Me-N.C. and Saint Ann's Robe-N.C.) belong to this draft. The pattern is different from Atwater #66, Guess Me.

223.
"9 Snow Balls". *On mussed brown paper. Sun. Sup. 1896.*

```
1   1   113   131 1   113   131 1   113   13   13   13   13   13   13
      242424         242424       24 24 24 24 24 24 24 24 24 24 24 24 24 24
1   1      13      1 1      13      1 1      13   13   13   13   13   13
6 6 2 6         6 6 2 6 6         6 6 2 6 6
```

224.
"The Nine Snow Balls for Two Colors". *On old cardboard.*

```
1 1 1 1 1   2           4         3  1 1 1 1 1 1   2           5 1
  6   6   3   1   2         3   1   2   6   6   3   1   2         4   4   4   4
          3   1   2   3   1   2                 3   1   2     1 1 1 1 1 1 1 1 1
6   4   6         3   11  2             6   4   6       3   1 2 2 6  6   6   6   6
```

```
            4 2         3  1 1 1 1 1 1   2                 4           3   1
4   4   4   4         3   1   2   6   6   3   1   2               3   1   2
1 1 1 1 1 1 1 1       3   1   2             3   1   2   3   1   2
  6   6   6   6 5 3 1   2         6   6   6         3   11  2
```

225.

```
                        1 3         1   3 8 2 4 8 8   2               1 3         1   3 8 8 2 4 8 8   2
  2 4   2 4   2 4   2 4   2 4   2 4       1   3   2   1     1   1   3   2         1   3   2   1     1     1   1   3
1 1 3 1 1 3 1 1 3 1 1 3 1 1 3 1 1 3 1   1   3   2               1   3   2     1   3   2
8     8     8     8     8     8     8 2 4   2             1 3   1         1   3 2 4   2       1     1 3   1
```

```
        1 3         1   3 8 8 2 4 8 8           1 3
  2                 1   3   2   1     1   1   3   2           2 4   2 4   2 4   2 4   2 4   2 4
1   3   2     1   3   2               1   3   2     1 1 3 1 1 3 1 1 3 1 1 3 1 1 3 1 1 3
  1   3 2 4   2         1     1 3   1         1   3 2 4 8   8     8     8     8     8
```

226.

```
                        1 3 5         2   1 3 5 1 3 5 1 3 5 1 3 5 1   3           2 4
  2 4       2 4       2 4       2 4       2   1   3   2 4 6     2 4 6       2   1   3
1 3 5 1 3 1 3 5 1 3 1 3 5 1 3 1 3 5 1 3 1 3 5   2   1   3                       2   1   3
2 4 6     2 4 6     2 4 6     2 4 6     2 4 6 2 4   1   3       2 4 6     2 4     2 4 6       2   1 3
```

```
        2   1 3 5 1 3 5 1 3 1 3 5 1 3 5 1   3           2 4
  2   1   3   2 4 6     2 4 6       2   1   3           2 4       2 4       2 4       2 4
  2   1   3                           2   1   3   1 3 5 1 3 1 3 5 1 3 1 3 5 1 3 1 3 5 1 3
1   3       2 4 6     2 4     2 4 6           2   1 3 5 2 4 6     2 4 6     2 4 6     2 4 6
```

223. Left to right, standard, condensed #3. Same as Rose #47, also Atwater #57, Nine Stars (or Snowballs) and Table.

224. Right to left, standard, condensed #3. In the 11th column from right, 1st line, number on top line should be a 3 and the number on the bottom line should be deleted. In the 51st column, the same configuration should repeat in reverse, but doesn't. Pattern is different from Atwater's Snowballs. It is the same as Rose #208 and 219, a flawed version of Granite State (Atwater #56).

225. Left to right, standard, condensed #3. A more-flawed version of #224.

226. Left to right, standard, condensed #2. Same as #224 and #225, but less flawed and with 4 wheels instead of 9.

227.
No name.

```
4                   4  4                        4  4  4  4  4                        4  4
        3  3  3  3  3  3  3  3  3           3  3  3  3  3              3  3  3  3  3  3  3
   2  2  2                 2  2  2  2  2  2  2  2              2  2  2           2  2  2  2  2  2
   1  1  1     1  1  1              1  1  1        1  1  1  1  1  1  1  1           1  1  1
```

```
         4  4  4  4
3  3  3  3  3
2  2
               1  1
```

228.
"Virginia Beauty". *Sun. Sup. 1896.*

```
      4  4        4  4        4  4        4  4        4  4        4  4  4  4
                                                                          3  3  3  3
2  2        2  2        2  2        2  2        2  2        2  2        2  2
  1  1  1  1  1  1  1  1  1  1  1  1  1  1  1  1  1  1  1  1  1  1  1  1  1  1
```

```
      4  4  4  4              4  4  4  4           4  4     4  4              4  4  4  4
            3  3  3  3              3  3  3  3  3  3           3  3  3  3
2  2              2  2  2  2              2  2              2  2  2  2
  1  1  1  1              1  1  1  1              1  1  1  1              1  1
```

```
         4  4  4  4              4  4  4  4              4  4           4  4  4
   3  3  3  3              3  3  3  3        3  3  3  3  3  3
2  2  2  2              2  2  2  2              2  2  2  2        2  2  2
1  1              1  1  1  1              1  1  1  1              1  1  1  1
```

```
4                 4  4  4
3  3  3  3
      2  2  2  2
            1  1  1  1
```

227. Right to left, standard, modern. Error: 3's in columns 18, 20, 59, 61 and 63 should apparently be 4's on the top row, but that change also introduces breaks in the tabby order. In treadling, the 3 in the 4th treadle should be a 4 (i.e., 1-4, not 1-3). If each treadle indicated is repeated to square, treadling is as drawn in. Pattern is a broken version of Atwater #1, Russian Diaper.

228. Left to right, standard, modern. Pattern is different from Atwater #240, Virginia Beauty. It is the same as Rose #136, a flawed diamond and table.

229.
"Wandering Vine #1".

```
                                    4   4   4   4   4   4   4   4   4   4   4   4   4   4
        3   3   3           3   3   3                   3   3   3           3   3   3
2   2   2   2   2   2   2   2   2   2   2   2   2   2
1   1   1               1   1           1   1   1   1   1   1               1   1               1   1   1


            4   4   4                   4   4   4                   4   4   4
        3   3   3   3               3   3   3   3               3   3   3   3
2   2   2   2                   2   2   2   2                   2   2   2   2
1   1                   1   1   1   1               1   1   1   1               1   1
```

231.
"WHƎƎLƎS". *Summer & Winter Wheal Draft. Groton 8th mo. 1825.*

```
        4 2             4 2                 8 6 4 2                                                              4 2         4 2
8 6 4 2             4 2             4 2                                          20 18 16 14 12 10 8 6 4 2       4 2
            4 2             4 2                             16 14 12 10 8 6 4 2
        4 2             4 2                 12 10 8 6 4 2
7   3   3   3   3   3   3   3   3   3   3   7   3   11      7   3   15      11      7   3   19      15      11      7   3   3   3   3
    5   1   1   1   1   1   1   1   1   1   1   5   1   9   5   1   13      9   5   1   17      13      9   5   1   1   1   1   1
```

```
            20 18 16 14 12 10 8 6 4 2       4 2         4 2         20 18 16 14 12 10 8 6 4 2
                                        4 2         4 2         4 2
                                                                                            12 10 8 6 4 2
16 14 12 10 8 6 4 2                                             16 14 12 10 8 6 4 2
15      11      7   3   19      15      11      7   3   3   3   3   3   3   3   19      15      11      7   3   15      11      7   3   11      7   3
13      9   5   1   17      13      9   5   1   1   1   1   1   1   1   17      13      9   5   1   13      9   5   1   9   5   1
```

```
    4 2                                                 8 6 4 2             4 2         4 2
4 2         20 18 16 14 12 10 8 6 4 2                                   4 2         4 2         8 6 4 2
                        16 14 12 10 8 6 4 2                         4 2         4 2             12 10 8 6 4 2
                                12 10 8 6 4 2                   4 2         4 2
3   3   19      15      11      7   3   15      11      7   3   11      7   3   7   3   3   3   3   3   3   3   3   3   7   3   11      7   3
    1   1   17      13      9   5   1   13      9   5   1   9   5   1   5   1   1   1   1   1   1   1   1   1   1   5   1   9   5   1
```

229. Left to right, standard, modern. Different from Atwater #39, Wandering Vine, which has reversals immediately before and after the stars that from the Cat Tracks. See Atwater #38, Cat Tracks, Snail Trail.

230. Not shown. Same as #229 (different draft mode).

231. Right to left, condensed #2. Summer & winter weave (4-thread blocks). Pattern is the same as Atwater #193-#194, Wheel of Fortune.

232.
"Wheels of Libenon".

Begin here to weave.   Begin to draw here

```
2 4           2 4 6 8                                            2 4      2 4 /  2 4
  2 4              2 4 6 8 10 12
    2 4                2 4 6 8 10 12 14 16
      2 4                  2 4 6 8 10 12 14 16 18 20    2 4    2 4    2 4 6 8 10 12 14 16 18 20
3  3  3  3  3  7  3  7  11  3  7  11  15  3  7  11  15  19  3  3  3  3  3  3  7  11  15  19
1  1  1  1  1  5  1  5  9   1  5  9   13  1  5  9   13  17  1  1  1  1  1  1  5  9   13  17
```

```
                    2 4 6 8          2 4          2 4                              2 4 6 8
            2 4 6 8 10 12                2 4          2 4              2 4 6 8 10 12 14 16
2 4 6 8 10 12 14 16              2 4          2 4         2 4 6 8 10 12
                    2 4          2 4          2 4 6 8
3  7  11  15  3  7  11  3  7  3  3  3  3  3  3  3  3  3  7  3  7  11  3  7  11  15  3  7
1  5  9   13  1  5  9   1  5  1  1  1  1  1  1  1  1  1  5  1  5  9   1  5  9   13  1  5
```

```
10 12 14 16 18 20    2 4    2 4    2 4 6 8 10 12 14 16 18 20                          2 4           O
                                        2 4 6 8 10 12 14 16                  2 4          O
                                           2 4 6 8 10 12          2 4    O
            2 4    2 4    2 4                                    2 4 6 8      2 4  O
11  15  19  3  3  3  3  3  3  7  11  15  19  3  7  11  15  3  7  11  3  7  3  3  3  3  3  O
9   13  17  1  1  1  1  1  1  5  9   13  17  1  5  9   13  1  5  9   1  5  1  1  1  1  1  O
```

233.
"Wheels of Time. Coverlet." *On mildewed soiled back of insurance calendar. 1910.*

```
5 5 2 1 2 5 5      2 2      2 2        5 5 2 1 2 5 5      2 2      2 2
  5  1  5    3  3    2 2  2 2    3  3   5  2  2  5 3  1  3 2     2    2 3   1 3
        3 3 1 3 3    2 2 2    3 3 1 3 3          3 3 1 3 3    2 2 2    3 3 1 3
5  2  2  5 3  1  3 2    2    2 3  1  3  5  1  5    3  3    2 2  2 2    3
```

232. Left to right, condensed #2. Summer & winter weave (4-thread blocks). Pattern is the same as #231 except drafted on different blocks.

233. Reads either way, standard, stacked. The final (right) 3's should move down one row to the bottom two rows. This draft and #234 are both flawed versions of Atwater #98, a Whig Rose and Lover's Knot combination. They are different from Atwater #101, Wheels of Time.

234.

```
1 1 1 3 1 1 3 1 1                1 3 1 3          1 3 1 3                    1 1 1 3 1 1 3 1 1
  8     2     8        2 4 6   2 4 6        2 4 2 4   2 4 2 4      2 4     2 4    8   2 4   2 4   8
            1 3 5 1 3 5 1 1 3 5 1 3 5    1 3 1 3 1 3      1 3 1 3 2 4 1 3 1 3
  8   2 4   2 4   8 2 4 6      2        2 4 6 2 4        2 4        2 4 2 4    1 3   2 4   8    2    8
```

```
                              1 3 1 3
2 4 6        2        2 4 6 1 3 1 3      2 4        2 4 2 4 6      2 2 4 6
1 3 5 1 3 5 1 1 3 5 1 3 5 2 4     1 3 1 3 1 3        1 3 5 1 3 1 1 3 5
    2 4 6   2 4 6            2 4 2 4   2 4 2 4          2 4
```

235.

"Whig Rose or Georgia Rose". *On green cardboard. Fairly recent.*

```
1 1 1 1 3 1      1 1 3 1      1 1 1 1 3 1
  6     6        4 2 6   4 2 6    6   6      6    4 2     6
            1 3 1      1 3 1          1 1 3 1 3 1 3 1 1 1
  6   6   4 2 6        6      4 2 6   6   4 2 6   4 2     4 2    6
```

Tread.
2-3 ·.
3-4 '.
2-3   each pair 13 times
3-4 ;
2-3 ·
1-2
1-4
1-2
1-4
1-2
2-3
3-4
1-4
1-2
1-4
3-4
2-3
1-2
1-4
1-2
1-4
1-2

236.

```
3 3 3 3 2      3 3 2    3 3 3 3 2
  3    3     2 3    2 3    3    3      6    2    6
          3 2      3 2         6 6 2 2 2 6 6
  3    3   2 3     3    2 3   3   2 6    2    2    6
```

234. Left to right, standard, condensed #3. Errors: in columns 14 and 15 from left of second line, all four numbers should be moved up one row to the top two rows. In columns 16 and 17 of second line, the 1 and 3 should move up to the top row. In column 33 of the second line, the 2 should be on the top row and the 1 on the bottom row. See pattern note on #233.

235. Right to left, standard, condensed #3. Different from Atwater Whig Rose.

236. Reads either way, standard, stacked. Pattern is a simple Lover's Knot, same as Rose #238 except larger. This is a rose-fashion treadling (remembering that 1 is the to shaft and 4 the bottom shaft in the draft).

237.
"Prim Rose and Diamonds".

4	4			4	4	4	4	4	4	4								4	4	4	4	4	4	4	4	4			
	3	3	3	3	3	3	3			3	3	3	3			3	3	3	3				3	3	3	3	3	3	3
	2	2										2	2	2	2	2	2	2									2	2	
				1	1									1	1	1				1	1	1							

238.
"Whig Rose Adaptation".

Repeat |→

4	4	4				4	4	4	4				4	4	4	4	4	4	4	4																						
3				3	3	3			3	3	3				3	3		3	3						3	3	3		3		3	3	3									
		2	2	2				2	2	2										2	2	2	2	2	2	2	2	2	2	2	2	2	2	2	2						
1	1	1				1				1	1	1			1				1	1	1	1			1		1							1	1	1					

|←

				4	4	4	4	4	
3	3	3				3	3		3
2	2	2	2	2	2				
		1	1	1	1			1	

Tread.
1-2
2-3
3-4
1-4
3-4
2-4
1-2
2-3
1-2
2-3
3-4
1-4
3-4

237. Reads either way, standard, modern. Almost the same as Rose #174 and Atwater #67, World's Wonder.

238. Right to left, standard, modern. Repeat is as indicated by arrows at beginning of first line and 10th column of second line. There is an error in treadling: the sixth treadle down should be 2-3. Pattern is the same as Rose #236 except smaller; or Atwater #69, simple Lover's Knot.

· 125 ·

239.

"Rose's Red Coverlet Pattern". *From sample of Mrs. La Farge. 20/1 course cotton white. Red wool. 6 repeats of pattern.*

Repeat A-B

← B → ← A. →

	4		4		4		4	4	4		4	4	4		4	4	4		4
3		3		3		3		3	3	3	3				3	3	3
2 2 2 2	2 2 2 2	2 2 2 2	2 2 2 2		2	2		2		2	2
1	1 1 1 1	1 1 1 1	1 1 1 1	1 1 1	1	1	1 1 1 1	1	1

← B

4 4	4 4 4	4	4 4		4		4		4		4		4
	3 3	3	3		3		3		3		3		3
	2	2	2	2 2 2	2 2 2 2	2 2 2 2	2 2 2 2	2 2 2 2
1 1 1 1	1	1 1 1	1 1 1 1	1 1 1 1	1 1 1 1	1 1 1 1	1 1 1 1	1 1 1

|End

	4 4 4	4	4
3		3	3	3 3
2 2 2		2	2
1 1	1 1 1	1	1

Tread.

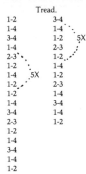

1-2	3-4
1-4	1-4
3-4	1-2 5X
1-4	2-3
2-3	1-2
1-2	1-4
1-4 5X	1-2
1-2	2-3
1-2	1-4
1-4	3-4
3-4	1-4
2-3	1-2
1-2	
1-4	
3-4	
1-4	
1-2	

240.

"Wide Worlds Wonder". *Sun. Sup. 1896.*

6 4 2		6 4 2 6 4 2 6 4 2		6 4 2 6 4 2 6 4 2 6 4 2 6 4 2 6 4 2					
	5 3 1		5 3 1	5 3 1	5 3 1	5 3 1	5 3 1	5 3 1	5 3 1	5 3 1	5 3 1
	4 2 6 4 2 4 2		4 2 6 4 2 4 2				4 2 6 4 2 4 2 6 4 2 4 2 6 4 2 4 2 6 4 2 4 2
5 3 1 3 1	3 1 5 3 1	5 3 1 3 1	3 1 5 3 1	5 3 1	5 3 1	5 3 1 3 1	3 1	3 1	3 1	3 1

	5 3 1	6 4 2 6 4 2 6 4 2 6 4 2 6 4 2 6 4 2		6 4 2 6 4 2 6 4 2		6 4 2 6 4 2 6 4 2 6 4 2 6 4 2
6 4 2		5 3 1	5 3 1	5 3 1	5 3 1	5 3 1		5 3 1	5 3 1	5 3 1
4 2	4 2				4 2 6 4 2 4 2		4 2 6 4 2 4 2			
3 1	3 1 5 3 1	5 3 1	5 3 1	5 3 1 3 1	3 1 5 3 1	5 3 1 3 1	3 1 5 3 1	5 3 1	5 3 1

| 5 3 1 | 6 4 2 | 5 3 1 | 5 3 1 |
| 6 4 2 4 2 5 3 1 4 2 6 4 2 4 2 6 4 2 |
| 3 1 | 3 1 | 3 1 |

239. Right to left, standard, modern. Repeat is as arrows indicate, from A to B on first two lines. Pattern is a variant of Rose #47. See also Rose #213 and #160.

240. Right to left, standard, condensed #2. Different from Atwater's World's Wonder, #67.

241.
"Wild Mountain Cucumber or Governors Garden". *Sun. Sup. 1896.*

```
  5 3 1 5 3 1            5 3 1     5 3 1     5 3 1     5 3 1     5 3 1     5 3 1     5 3 1     5 3 1     5 3 1
6 4 2 6 4 2                6 4 2 6 4 2 6 4 2 6 4 2 6 4 2 6 4 2 6 4 2 6 4 2 6 4 2 6 4 2 6 4 2 6 4 2 6 4 2 6 4 2 6 4 2 6 4 2 6 4 2 6 4 2 6 4 2
5 3 1             5 3 1 5 3 1     5 3 1     5 3 1     5 3 1     5 3 1     5 3 1     5 3 1     5 3 1     5 3 1
        6 4 2 6 4 2
```

```
5 3 1              5 3 1 5 3 1         5 3 1 5 3 1            5 3 1 5 3 1            5 3 1 5 3 1
6 4 2 6 4 2      6 4 2 6 4 2         6 4 2      6 4 2 6 4 2      6 4 2 6 4 2      6 4 2      6 4 2 6 4 2
    5 3 1 5 3 1 5 3 1          5 3 1 5 3 1 5 3 1          5 3 1 5 3 1 5 3 1          5 3 1 5 3 1 5 3 1          5 3 1 5 3 1
        6 4 2         6 4 2 6 4 2         6 4 2 6 4 2          6 4 2          6 4 2 6 4 2         6 4 2 6 4 2          6 4 2
```

```
    5 3 1 5 3 1            5 3 1 5 3 1             5 3 1
        6 4 2 6 4 2      6 4 2 6 4 2         6 4 2
6 4 2         5 3 1 5 3 1 5 3 1          5 3 1 5 3 1 6 4 2
5 3 1 6 4 2         6 4 2          6 4 2 6 4 2      5 3 1 6 4 2
```

242.
"Winter and Summer". *On a small piece of brown paper. Looks as if it was used a good deal.*

```
4 4      4      8 4 8 4 8 4 8 4 8 4 8 4 8 4 8 4 8      4      4
  1 1          1 1   1   1   1   1   1   1   1   1 1         1 1
    4 4   4 4                                    4 4   4 4
1       1 1 1      1   1   1   1   1   1   1   1      1 1 1
```

241. Right to left, standard, condensed #2. Different from Atwater #23, Governor's Garden. Similar to Rose #74 and Atwater #17 and #20, John Walker and Lily of the Valley.

242. Reads either way, standard, condensed #1. Winter and Summer is the pattern name, not the weave (it is overshot). See also Rose #172 and #214. Similar to Atwater #73; Burnham #258-#264, Monmouth.

243.

"From Tenn. Wisconsin Beauty". *On dirty brown paper. "Best one" written on this. Evidently sent him recently.*

```
    4 2 8 6      6 8 4 2              4 2 8 6    6 8 4 2
3 1         1 3 1 1   3 1 3 1     3 1    3 1 3 1   1 3 1 1   3 1 3 1   3 1   3 1   3 1   3 1   3 1
4 2         4 2       4 2 4 2 4 2 4 2        4 2             4 2 8 4 2 8 4 2 8 4 2 8 4 2 8 6 4 2
    3 1 1      1         3 1     3 1     1         1         1     1     1     1     1     7 5 3 1
```

244.

```
    2 5 6    6 5 2         2 5 6    6 5 2
2 2    6 2 6   2 2   2   2 2    6 2 6   2 2   2   2   2   2   2
2      2        2 2 2 2 2    2        2 5 2 5 2 5 2 5 2 5 2 5
    5        5      2 2     5        5      5     5     5     5     5     5
```

245.

"The Wonder of the Forest". *Sun. Sup. 1896. Dirty.*

```
2 4 6      2 4      2 4      2 4      2 4 6    2 4 6    2 4 6    2 4 6    2 4 6      2 4      2 4
1 3 5                                1 3 5 1 3 1 3 5 1 3 1 3 5 1 3 1 3 5 1 3 1 3 5
    2 4 6    2 4 6    2 4 6    2 4 6      2 4      2 4      2 4      2 4      2 4 6    2 4 6
    1 3 5 1 3 1 3 5 1 3 1 3 5 1 3 1 3 5                                    1 3 5 1 3 1 3 5 1 3
```

```
                              |    12X    |
    2 4      2 4 6    2 4 6      2 4 6    2 4 6      2 4 6
         1 3 5 1 3 1 3 5      1 3 5 1 3 1 3 5      1 3 5 1 3
2 4 6    2 4 6    2 4      2 4 6      2 4      2 4 6      2 4
1 3 5 1 3 1 3 5         1 3 5              1 3 5
```

---

243. Right to left, standard, condensed #3. In the 50th and 51st columns from right, the 1 and 3 should be on the third row up, not the lowest. See Rose #26. A Double Chariot Wheel or Church Windows pattern.

244. Reads either way, standard, stacked. See Rose #26. Identical to Atwater #84, Double Chariot Wheel or Church Window.

245. Left to right, standard, condensed #2. Same as Rose #164. Similar to Atwater #130, Missouri Check.

·APPENDIX·

Drawdowns of most of the Rose drafts are presented here. They were generated by Carol Strickler on an Apple 2+ computer using "Weft-Writer" software written by Stuart Strickler. The drawdowns are vignettes; they don't necessarily represent the entire draft, and do not necessarily start on the first thread. Their purpose is to give you a visual image of the pattern; if you plan to weave one of the drafts, be sure and analyze and balance it before you begin.

The drafts have been treadled "as drawn in" unless a treadling is included with the draft, or unless otherwise noted. In some cases the treadling has been compressed so that more of the repeat can be shown; thus some motifs are laterally elongated. A few drafts that were virtual duplicates of others have been omitted; weave structures such as huckaback that do not read well as drawdowns have also been left out.

1.

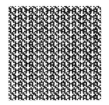

2.

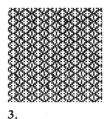

3.

4. Treadled as given.

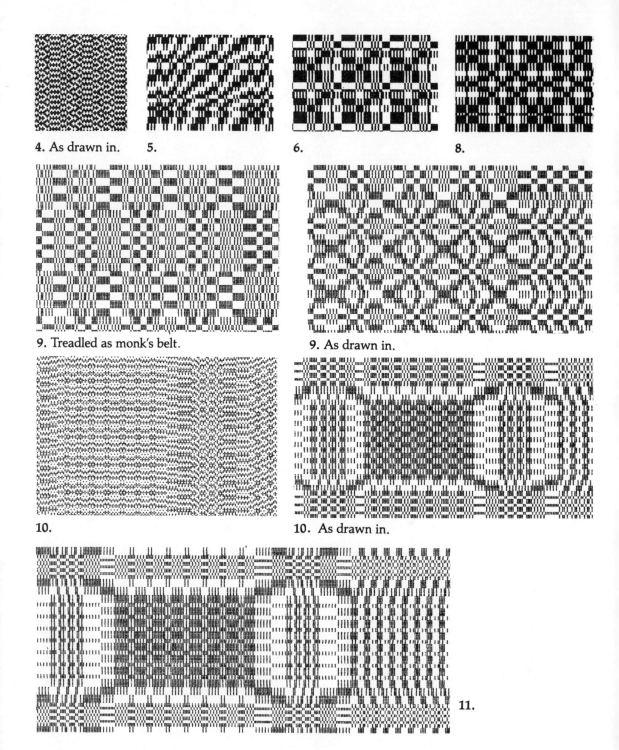

4. As drawn in.   5.   6.   8.

9. Treadled as monk's belt.

9. As drawn in.

10.

10. As drawn in.

11.

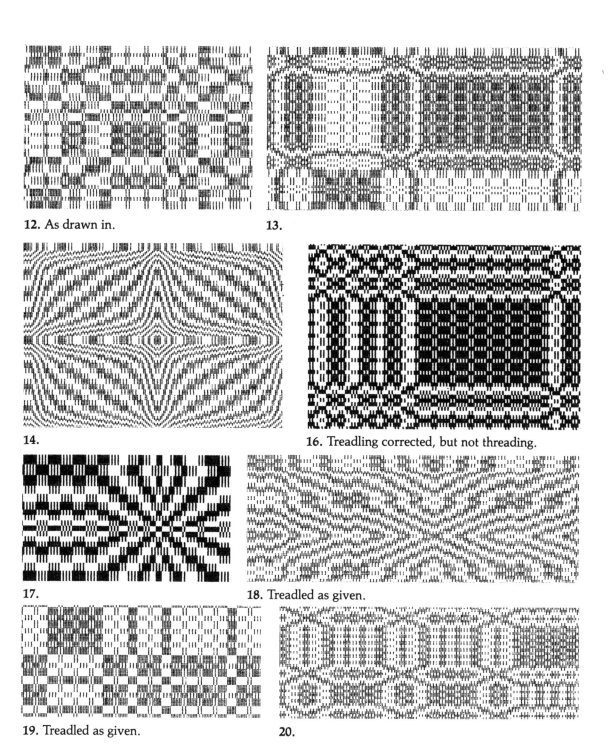

12. As drawn in.

13.

14.

16. Treadling corrected, but not threading.

17.

18. Treadled as given.

19. Treadled as given.

20.

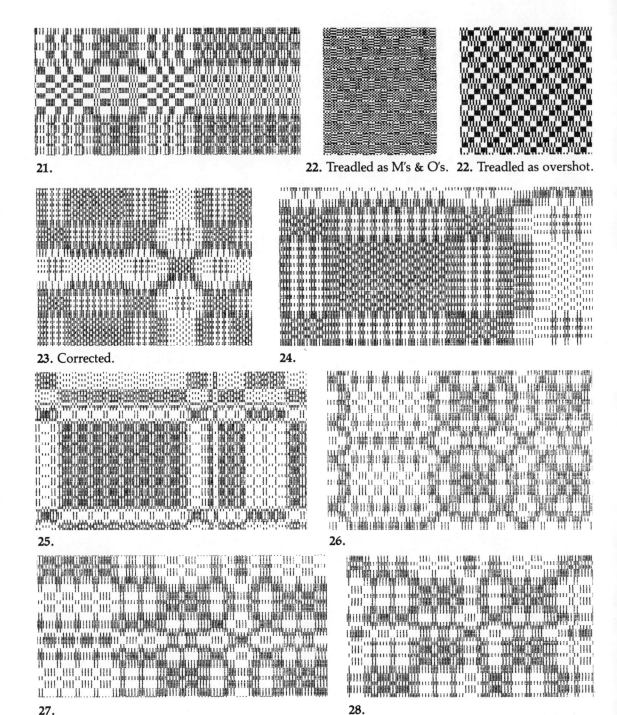

21.

22. Treadled as M's & O's. 22. Treadled as overshot.

23. Corrected.

24.

25.

26.

27.

28.

29.

30.

31.

32.

33.

34.

35.

36.

37.

38.

39.

40. Block draft.

41. Treadled as given. **42.**

43. As drawn in. **43.** Treadled as given. **44.**

45.

46.

47.

48.

48. Treadled rose-fashion.

49.

50. Block drawdown.

51. Block, as drawn in.

51. Block, rose-fashion.

51. Block, tied B, A, C-D, C.

55.

56. As drawn in.

56. Rose-fashion.

59. Block.

60.

62. Block.

64.

65. Block.

66.

67.

68. Block.

69.

70. Block.

71.

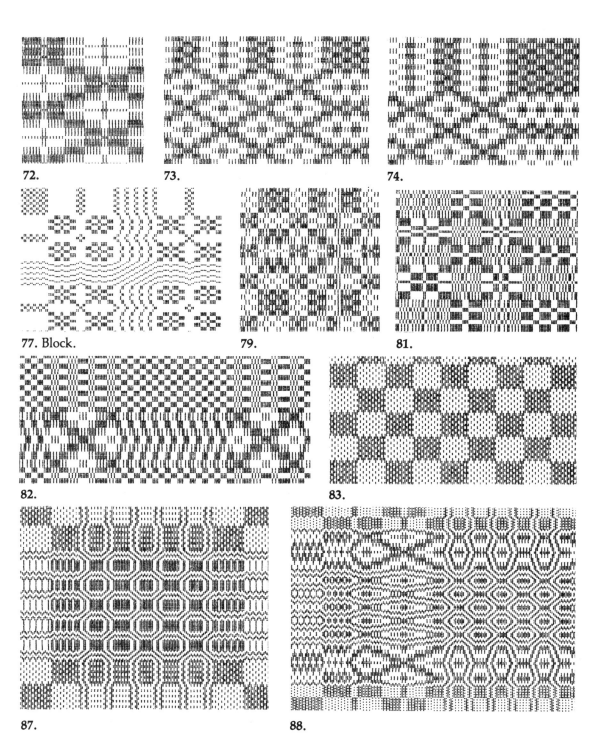

72.

73.

74.

77. Block.

79.

81.

82.

83.

87.

88.

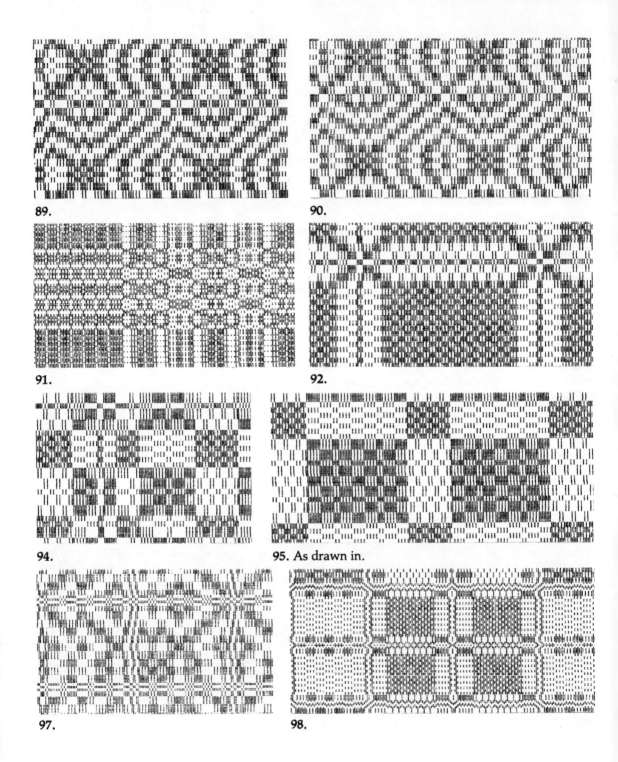

89.

90.

91.

92.

94.

95. As drawn in.

97.

98.

100.

101. As drawn in.

102.

104.

105.

106. Treadling corrected, but not threading.

107. As drawn in, not as given.

109. As drawn in, not as given.

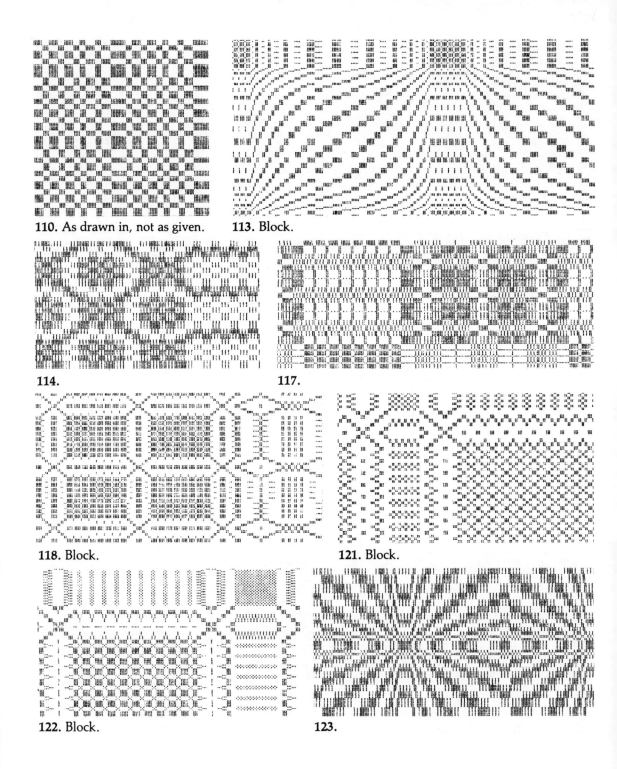

110. As drawn in, not as given.   **113.** Block.

114.   **117.**

118. Block.   **121.** Block.

122. Block.   **123.**

124.

127.

128.

129.

130.

131.

132. Assuming the first line is A&B blocks.

134.

· 141 ·

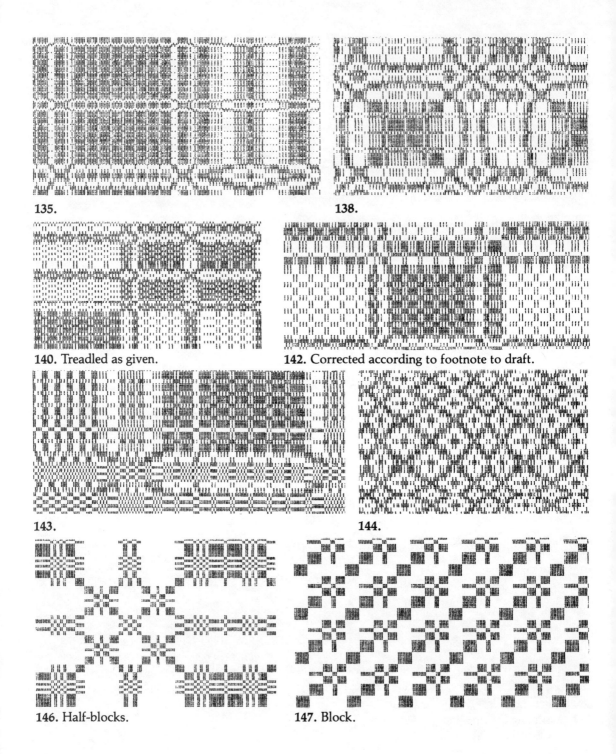

135.

138.

140. Treadled as given.

142. Corrected according to footnote to draft.

143.

144.

146. Half-blocks.

147. Block.

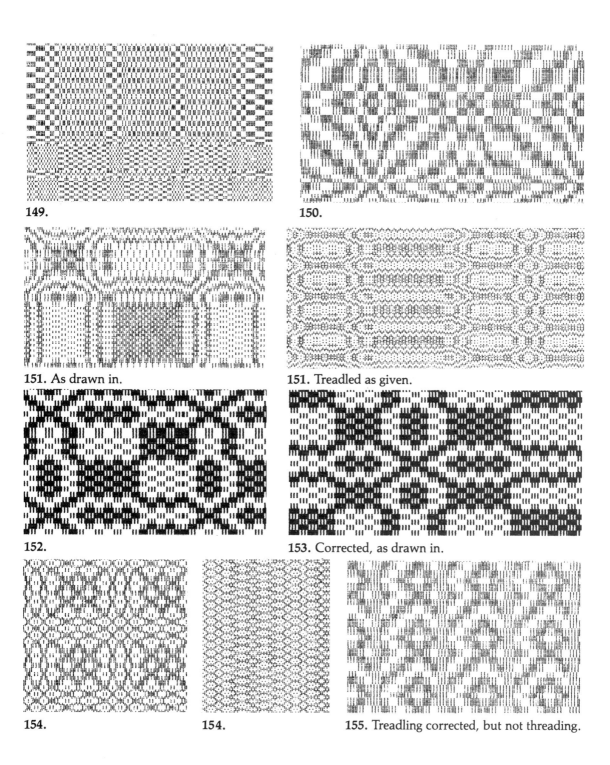

149.

150.

151. As drawn in.

151. Treadled as given.

152.

153. Corrected, as drawn in.

154.

154.

155. Treadling corrected, but not threading.

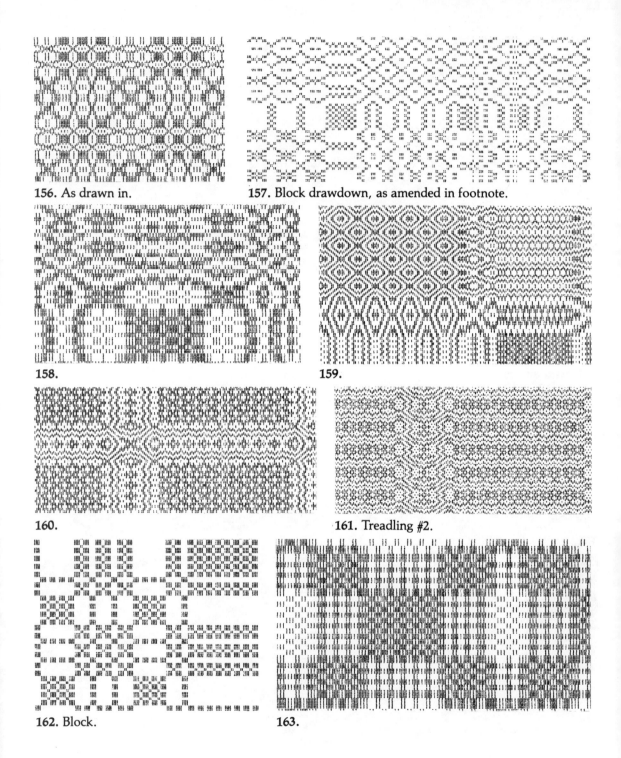

156. As drawn in.

157. Block drawdown, as amended in footnote.

158.

159.

160.

161. Treadling #2.

162. Block.

163.

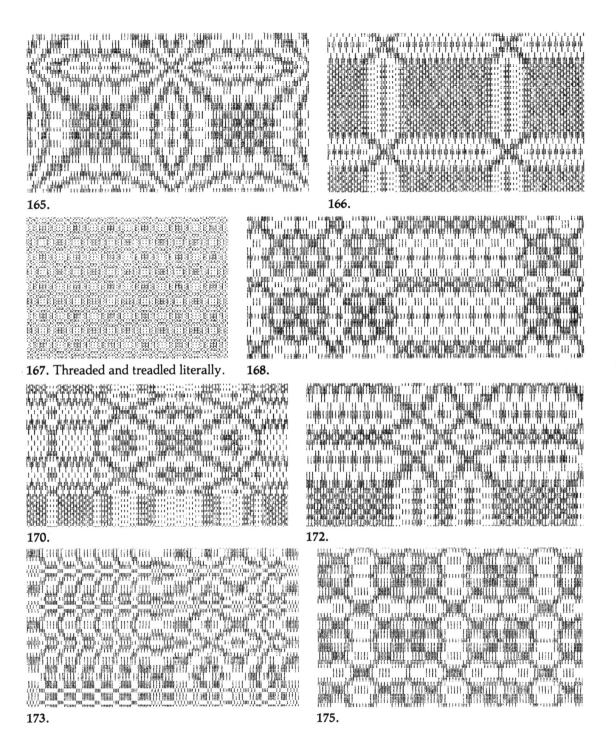

165.

166.

167. Threaded and treadled literally.

168.

170.

172.

173.

175.

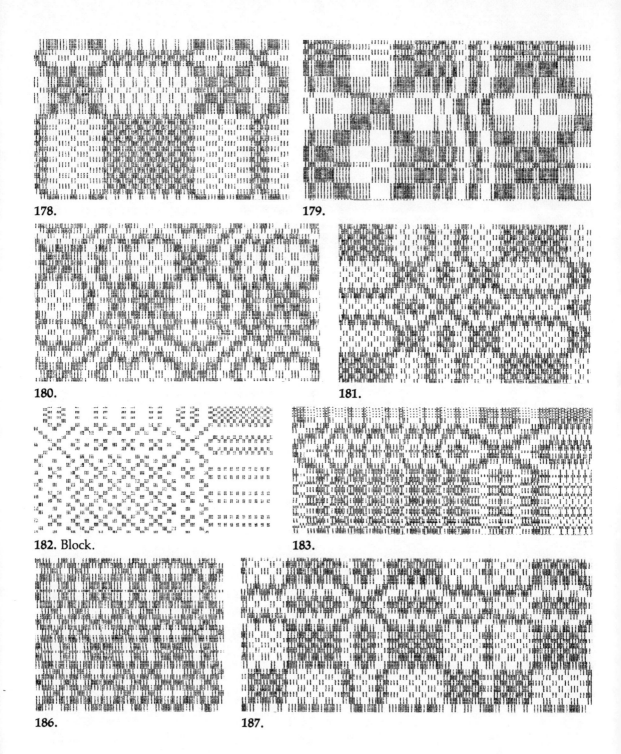

178.

179.

180.

181.

182. Block.

183.

186.

187.

· 146 ·

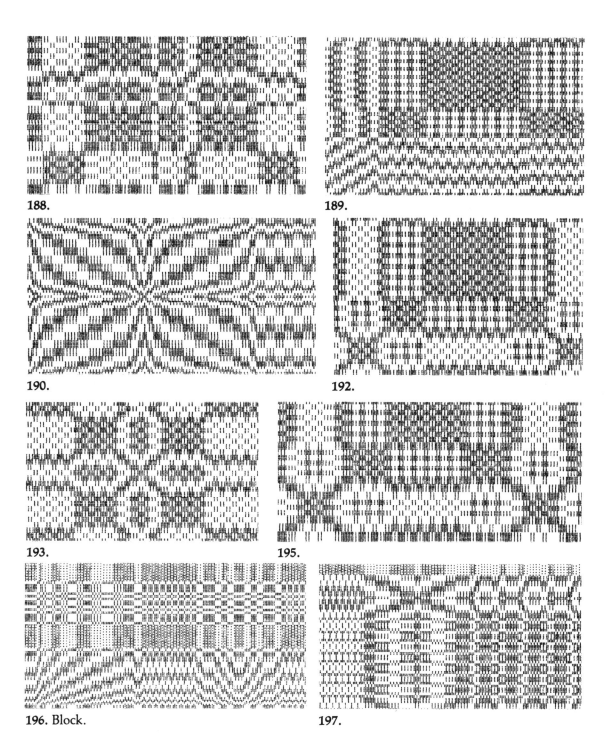

188.

189.

190.

192.

193.

195.

196. Block.

197.

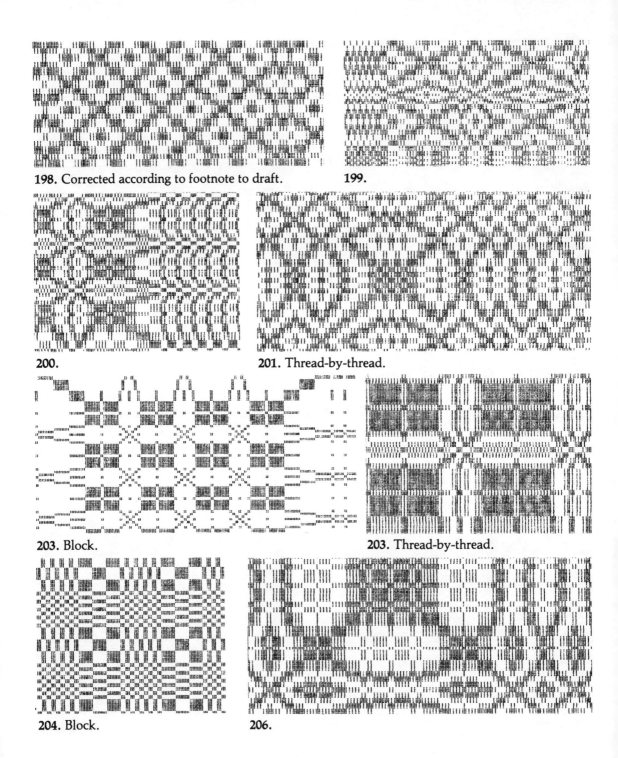

198. Corrected according to footnote to draft.

199.

200.

201. Thread-by-thread.

203. Block.

203. Thread-by-thread.

204. Block.

206.

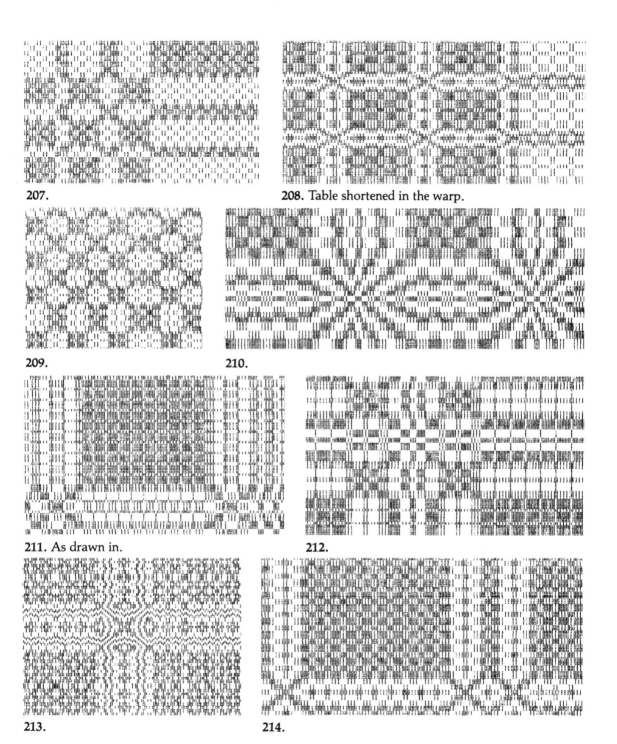

207.

208. Table shortened in the warp.

209.

210.

211. As drawn in.

212.

213.

214.

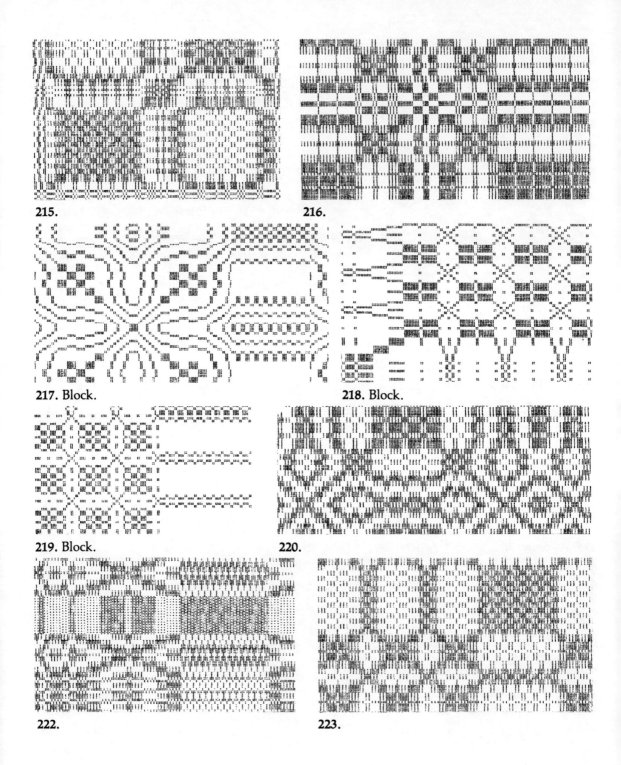

215.

216.

217. Block.

218. Block.

219. Block.

220.

222.

223.

224.

226.

228.

227. As drawn in.

229 & 230. As drawn in.

231.

233.

235. As drawn in.

236. As drawn in.

237.

238. Rose-fashion.

238. As drawn in.

239. As drawn in.

239. Treadled as given.

240.

241. Thread-by-thread.

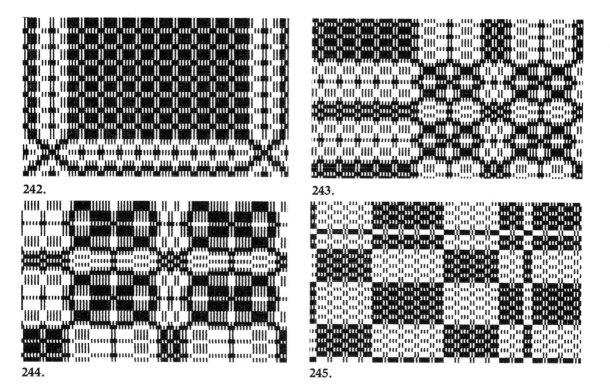

242.

243.

244.

245.

BIBLIOGRAPHY

Allen, Laura. Draft Collection. Private Library.

Atwater, Mary Meigs. *The Shuttle-Craft Book of American Handweaving*. New York: The Macmillan Co., 1947.

Burnham, D.K. & H.B. *Keep Me Warm One Night*. Toronto and Buffalo: University of Toronto Press, 1975.

Burnham, D.K. *Warp and Weft*. Toronto: Royal Ontario Museum, 1980.

Barlow, A. *The History and Principles of Weaving*. London: Sampson, Low, Marston, Searle, and Rivington, 1879.

Bronson, J. & R. *The Domestic Manufacturer's Assistant, And Family Directory*. Utica: William Williams, 1817.

Campbell, Mary M. *The New England Butt'ry Shelf Almanac*, New York: The World Publishing Co., 1970.

Chapin, Howard M. *Sachems of the Narragansetts*. Providence: The Rhode Island Historical Society, 1931.

Correspondence of Elsie Maria Babcock Rose. Private Library.

Correspondence of Emily Beals. Private Library.

Correspondence of William Henry Harrison Rose. Private Library.

Davison, Marguerite Porter. *A Handweaver's Pattern Book*. Swarthmore, Pennsylvania, 1955.

-----. *A Handweaver's Source Book*. Chester, Pennsylvania: John Spencer, Inc., 1953.

Earle, Alice Morse. *Home Life in Colonial Days*. New York: The Macmillan Co., 1948.

-----. *In Old Narragansett*. New York: Charles Scribner's Sons, 1898.

Gordy, W.F. *A History of the United States*. New York: Charles Scribner's Sons, 1898.

Greene, E.B. *The American Nation: A History* Vol. 6, Provincial America. New York and London: Harper and Brothers, 1904.

Huden, J.C. *Indian Place Names of New England*. New York: Museum of the American Indian, Heye Foundation, 1962.

Kaye, A.G. "Weaver Rose, A New Perspective". *Shuttle, Spindle and Dyepot*, Vol. VIII, no. 2, Spring, 1977.

Pariseau, G.D. "Weaver Rose of Rhode Island". *Handweaver and Craftsman*, Vol. 6, no. 1, Winter, 1954-1955.

Providence Evening Bulletin, Feb. 17, 1939 "R.I. State College Girls Use Oaken Loom of Weaver Rose".

Providence Journal, Oct. 8, 1905, p. 24.

Providence Journal, March 2, 1923, p. 17.

Rider, Sidney S. *The Lands of Rhode Island As They Were Known To Cauncounicus And Miantunnomu When Roger Williams Came In 1636*. Providence, Rhode Island: Published by Author, 1904.

Sprigg, J. *Domestick Beings*. New York: Alfred A. Knopf, 1984.

Tyler, L.G. *The American Nation: A History*. Vol. 4, England in America. New York and London: Harper and Brothers, 1904.

The Weaver's Enterprise. Vol. 1, no. 1. Battle Creek, Michigan: W.H. Kynett, M.D., Editor and Publisher, 1893.

The Weaver's Herald and Household Magazine. Vol. VIII, nos. 1 & 2. Lyons, Kansas, 1899. The Wonderly Co., publisher.

Wilson, S.T. & Kennedy, D.F. *Of Coverlets*. Nashville, Tennessee: Tunstede, 1983.

Young, Helen Daniels. *Drawing on the Diagonal*. Brewster, Massachusetts: Two Cape Cod Weavers, 1982.

-----. *A Study of the Relationship Between Borders and Patterns*. Brewster, Massachusetts; Two Cape Cod Weavers, 1982.